DESIGNING FURNITURE

Bench by Kenton Hall, Providence, R.I. (Photo by Dean Powell.)

DESIGNING FURNITURE

from concept to shop drawing: a practical guide

SETH STEM

edited by Laura Tringali

The Taunton Press

FRONT COVER: Ménage à Trois, one of a series of benches by Mitch Ryerson of Cambridge, Mass. (Photo by Dean Powell.)

BACK COVER, TOP LEFT: Cloud Table by Everett Bramhall of Cambridge, Mass. (Photo by Seth Stem.)

BACK COVER, BOTTOM LEFT: Highboy by Joe Duke of New York, N.Y. (Photo courtesy Gallery of Applied Art, New York, N.Y.)

BACK COVER, RIGHT: Vanity stool by Charles Swanson of Providence, R.I. (Photo by Charles Swanson.)

©1989 by The Taunton Press, Inc.
All rights reserved

First printing: March 1989

International Standard Book Number: 0-942391-02-0

Library of Congress Catalog Card Number: 88-51784

Printed in the United States of America

A FINE WOODWORKING Book

FINE WOODWORKING® is a trademark of The Taunton Press, Inc., registered in the U.S. Patent and Trademark Office.

TAUNTON
BOOKS & VIDEOS

...by fellow enthusiasts

The Taunton Press
63 South Main Street
Newtown, Connecticut 06470

acknowledgments

Many individuals have contributed in some way to the creation of this book, and to them I extend my sincerest thanks. I am especially grateful to all the furniture designers and makers who cooperated with my efforts to obtain photographs—I wish there had been space to use them all.

Special thanks also are due Christopher Monkhouse, Curator of Decorative Arts at the Museum of Art, Rhode Island School of Design, who gave me the confidence to write this book during a very brief discussion several years ago. Also at RISD I would like to thank Micky Ackerman, John Dunnigan, Tage Frid and Rosanne Somerson, with whom I have taught, for helping to create a most stimulating design atmosphere, for sharing their points of view about design and for the discussions and arguments we have had over the years.

My appreciation to the Gallery at Workbench in New York City, directed by Vanessa Lynn, as well as to the Society of Arts and Crafts in Boston, particularly Julie Mansfield—both gave me free access to their slide collections. I would also like to express my appreciation to Dean Powell, whose excellent photography has captured many of the moods and images of the furniture pieces shown in this book.

Finally, my special gratitude to Laura Tringali, my editor and now good friend, who supported and nurtured, directed, corrected and questioned me during the writing and development of all the chapters of this book.

I dedicate this book to my son, David, whose provocative creative spirit has enriched my life.

introduction

For the furniture maker who works in wood, the romance of the making is often a gratifying and creative experience. Involvement with the material and tools, joinery and finishes can provide tremendous joy and satisfaction, and after the work is complete, a piece of furniture exists that is lovingly presented to family, friends or the marketplace. But I can't even begin to count the number of times that a woodworker has proudly shown me a photograph of a table, chair or chest that is improperly proportioned, badly detailed or just plain ugly. Usually the maker has a great attachment to the work and can't see its shortcomings for the pride of workmanship. And the piece *is* worked beautifully—tight joints, beautiful finish, good use of wood. It never fails to break my heart that there isn't more of a balance in these cases between careful construction and careful design.

Obviously, even the best craftsmanship can't compensate for poor design. But the very idea of original design can be so intimidating that some furniture makers leave the whole issue to a subconscious muse and simply hope for the best. The situation is made worse by the scarcity of published material on design—there are plenty of books and magazine articles on successful designers and their work, but very little has been written on the processes they use to achieve their goals.

When my editor and I began to work out the structure of this book, we immediately agreed that it must be different in that regard. Our aim was to provide a toolbox of ideas with which readers having a serious interest in furniture making but little or no design background could craft visually pleasing and exciting furniture. Further, we wanted to give readers a skeleton methodology to which they could cling either when facing a dearth of ideas or when in danger of being overwhelmed by too many divergent ones. Our goal was to provide a relatively straightforward design process that would allow beginners to build confidence as they made real the furniture of their dreams.

A straightforward process, however, implies a great degree of linearity. I am afraid that design as practiced by designers is anything but linear. Depending on the idea, the designer, the client and in-fluences that sometimes seem as arbitrary as the phases of the moon, the path from idea to finished piece can be infinitely varied. For instance, I recently had a student who designed and built a very different sort of chair by welding ¼-in. dia. steel rods together into a three-dimensional composition. Not one drawing was done for the project. The design evolved from a hands-on study of how a steel-rod structure could support the human body. Pieces were welded on, others were cut off, and still others were added at different points and angles to provide rigidity, comfort or visual interest. This chair developed spontaneously in a most interesting visual, functional and structural way, beyond what most designers could plan or project on paper.

Another student chose to work through a meticulously structured design process to create his chair. He began by formulating a concept for an adjustable seat and back. Then he made drawings, models and mockups, researched materials, studied seat and back angles, and planned out the structure and mechanisms. He performed tests using samples of actual materials and then built the chair from detailed measured drawings. The result was a well-engineered chair, beautiful and elegant and as successful as the steel-rod chair, though no two design approaches could have had less in common.

This point is important because I wouldn't want readers to think that the method presented in this book is the one true path toward good furniture design. It's a smooth path and a wide one, and the one I follow myself most of the time, but the linearity of its steps is not necessarily workable for every design—or every designer. In many cases, it will seem more reasonable to reverse steps or even skip a step or two. I therefore urge readers to follow the path but also to follow their good common sense and to listen to their creative urges and intuition. Trust that if something feels right, there is a good chance that it will be right.

The design process presented in this book is somewhat formal. There are structured exercises to produce different forms, visual references, icons, an array of proportioning systems and a visual vocabulary to master. This is quite different from the intuitive approach to design taught in many colleges and taken by most self-taught designers. I don't wish to imply that excellent pieces cannot be achieved by the intuitive method—in fact, some of the freshest designs are produced this way. I believe, however, that a more structured approach can open a designer's eyes to new possibilities and add a new degree of dynamism to a piece. In addition, for the beginner not quite comfortable with the language of design, there is no doubt that a sense of structure lends a great deal of reassurance and builds confidence.

Part of our society is open to new ideas and change, while another faction relates best to the familiar. Designers can affect both of these attitudes, but I feel real creative progress comes only when risks are taken and innovation is courted, because only then is there growth that impacts on the visual and functional qualities of things that we encounter in day-to-day living. Many furniture designers are involved in this quest for newness, but in a variety of ways. They look for new styles, new materials and production methods, and innovative ways to deal with function. Recently, furniture has even begun to be viewed as an art form, which greatly widens the range of visual issues a designer can legitimately explore. It is my belief that the opportunity has never been greater for furniture designers to become involved in work of an adventuresome nature.

Design isn't usually an easy task. It requires a lot of thought, work and indeed trial and error to produce a piece of high visual and functional quality. I hope readers will find this book a worthy contribution to the effort.

Seth Stem
Providence, R.I.
March 1989

contents

THE DESIGN PROCESS

Design starts with inspiration, the very beginning of an idea. The inspiration may come from viewing furniture in a shop, or from sources as diverse as the form of a beautiful building on the street or the construction of a suit of armor in a museum. A less tangible catalyst might also be responsible, such as the perception of a commonly experienced need. The idea resulting from such inspiration may be as simple as the thought that it would be nice to make something for personal use, or as specific as a commission for a client. But in any idea's transition from sketch to object, many design and technical issues must be faced and many decisions have to be made. There is persistent danger of being intimidated and confused by too many choices, or, in some cases, by not understanding the full range of choices. In successful design, there is a fine line between adhering to the initial idea and experimenting with creative options to strengthen it. Overworking a piece can obscure and confuse its original intent, yet working it too little can leave it underdeveloped, and the resulting object neither fulfills its intended function nor realizes its full aesthetic potential.

In approaching design, it is useful to establish a process to help organize the work, eliminate oversights and lend a bit of logic to what can be a frustratingly subjective exercise. What follows is a summary of the design process I use for myself. The first two components are explored in the first chapter of this section; the rest are discussed in the second chapter.

1. Conceptualization—Here you create a concept. This evolves from the initial idea and a "problem statement," which is your plan of how to proceed during design.

2. Research—Research all aspects of the problem to collect as much information as possible.

3. Design development—Develop the design to a point where the object can be built.

4. Implementation—Implement the design (construct the piece).

5. Evaluation—Evaluate the completed project.

6. Presentation—Present the piece in a professional, informative way.

Though this is the process I follow, don't think that it is the only one to use. One of the wonderful things about design is that the experience can be as individual as the designer (or the project). Design can be approached in many ways, depending on the background of the designer, the requirements of the particular design and the complexity of the piece.

The concept of this piece was based on a table's reaction to earthquake—hence the shifting planes of the top and leg blocks. Earthquake Table was designed and made by Tom Loeser of Cambridge, Mass. (Photo by Tom Loeser.)

conceptualization and research

The first task is to craft the initial idea, however it was inspired, into a strong concept. A concept is a well-defined, formally stated idea that describes the main issues (whether structural, functional or visual) the piece will address. In design, this stage is called "conceptualization." To create a concept, you must first develop a "problem statement," which is simply a definition of the issues to be investigated in the design. A problem statement can be simple or complex, ranging from "to create a dining-room table that complements existing furniture and will seat the entire family plus occasional guests" to "a dining-room table that reflects the vertical lines of the surrounding architecture and folds to minimal size when not in use." The concepts developed from these problem statements might be "an extension table for ten people derivative of the Art Deco style in form and materials" and "a drop-leaf table that accentuates verticality in both the open and closed positions by using vertical images of forms on the legs (for verticality in the extended position) and on the folded table surface (for the closed mode)."

The point of a strong concept is to give direction to the development of the piece, while at the same time allowing the maximum evolution of the idea. The photos at left and on the facing page illustrate pieces designed around a concept. A strong concept is especially important if there are restrictions on the design. If, for example, midway through the construction of a dining table you long to paint the legs shocking pink instead of leaving them natural maple, you may be able to change your direction and create a dynamic new look provided you have the latitude to indulge your creativity. But if your concept specifies that your piece must blend with a roomful of Colonial furniture, you'll be forced to question your creative urge before picking up the paintbrush. You may decide that pink legs would make an important visual statement, but you might also decide to save the color for another piece. In any case, your decision will be a product of deliberate thought, not of whim or the late hour of the night. In this way, a strong concept allows the designer to establish a framework within which to settle any questions and

FACING PAGE: The concept of this piece was to create a fantasy landscape within a children's bed. Co-designed by Lee Schuette of Kittery Point, Maine, and Linda Schiwall-Gallo of Ashfield, Mass., the bed uses simple construction in line with the visual message. (The picket fence, for example, is nailed together, not joined.) Even the bedspread supports the concept. The foliage of the tree next to the bed tilts 90° to form a night table. (Quilt by Ann Schiwall; Photo by Steven Sloman.)

ABOVE: The concept behind this Perch Chair, designed by Dick and Carol Bourne of Davis, Calif., was to transfer the weight of the child to the table edge to anchor and support the seat securely. (Photo by Seth Stem, courtesy Country Workshop, Cambridge, Mass.)

RIGHT: The concept of this piece by Tom Loeser of Cambridge, Mass., was to make a folding chair that had strong visual impact both when open and closed, and that when folded could be a wall sculpture. The geometric composition and the separation of faces and edges through color and painted patterns give the chair a strong, three-dimensional quality. The edge patterns disappear when the chair is folded, leaving only the striped surfaces exposed. (Photo by Dean Powell.)

A PAGE FROM THE AUTHOR'S SKETCHBOOK

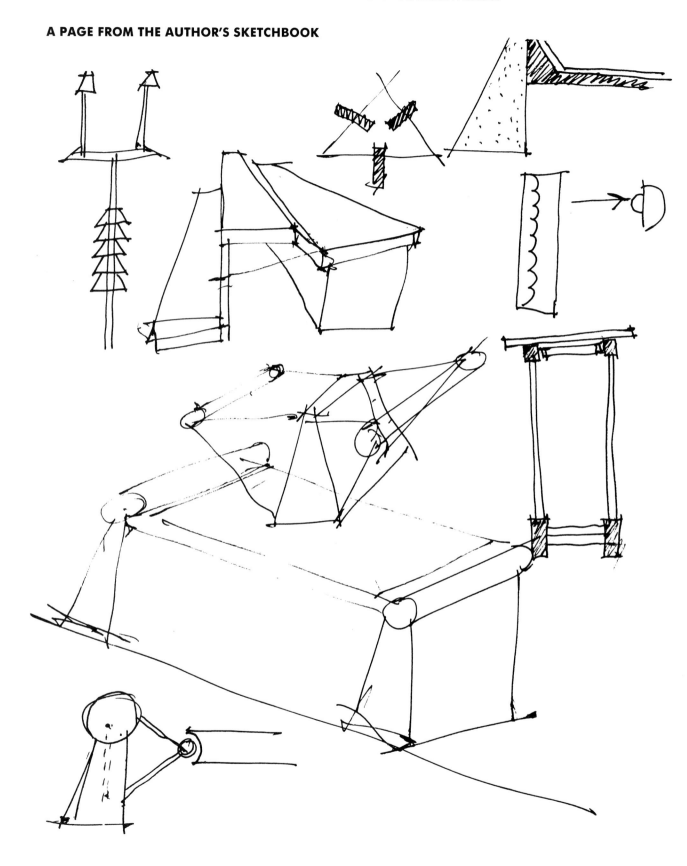

problems that may arise in the development and construction of a piece.

We've all had innovative ideas that pop effortlessly into our heads while driving a car or taking a shower, and these can often be molded into strong concepts with a bit more thought. But what if your idea simply expresses the desire to create some sort of furniture? How do you then draft a problem statement? Function is a good place to start, but it may not be enough to state, "I want to build a comfortable chair." Design may be more fruitful if you can pinpoint an aesthetic or structural issue you'd like to investigate, or a very specific functional one, such as "a chair that supports the occupant in at least three different positions." If you have been keeping a journal of ideas as they arise, discovering interesting aesthetic, structural or functional issues might simply consist of turning its pages until you see something that sparks your imagination.

Whenever I have a new idea for a piece of furniture, I quickly sketch it and any variations, including top, front and end views. Sometimes I'll even enlarge and render an area in three dimensions to capture important details. I toss these sketches in a file if I don't have a sketchbook with me, and when I'm working on a new project I refer to this first. Over the years I've collected hundreds of ideas. Most don't stand the test of time, unfortunately, and even many of the good ideas never go anywhere. Every few years the materials, processes and styles I'm interested in change, and new ideas replace the old. Still, these quick sketches, like the ones on the facing page, have often proved useful.

If you have no journal, then plan to begin one. In the meantime, approach conceptualization by studying objects that attract your attention at home, in stores or, in fact, anywhere. Sometimes I look to craft works in other media for ideas, or to painting and sculpture. These sources take the designer out of the traditional context of furniture structure, process and materials and open up new possibilities. Any object in our environment, any event we view or article we read may suggest an idea and thus a furniture concept. Look at form, structure, connections between materials, color, texture, composition and ornamentation, the way the object functions and its character. Then see how these elements can be related to your design. (See also the section on visual references and icons, pp. 34-40.) For example, at right is a sketch of a table concept based on the 19th-century Albanian woman's dress coat shown below it. The epaulets, which cover the shoulders and arms, were the main point of inspiration. This element was translated into the idea of protective coverings or shields on the table legs.

TWO VIEWS OF A TABLE-LEG DESIGN

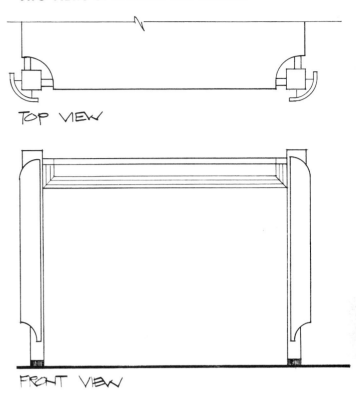

The legs of the table design in the drawing were inspired by the epaulets of the 19th-century Albanian woman's dress coat shown in the photo. (Photo courtesy Museum of Art, Rhode Island School of Design, gift of Mrs. Phillip Adams.)

the role of research in design

You can also look at like objects for inspiration. In furniture design this translates into researching existing furniture in books and magazines and attending museum and gallery shows. (In this case, research precedes conceptualization as the first step in the design process.)

When research is directly responsible for a concept, the designer usually assimilates the information and focuses it in a new direction, bringing his or her own point of view to the process. For example, the chests shown in the photo below refer visually to the work of Jacques-Emile Ruhlmann, a well-known furniture designer of the Art Deco period. In Ruhlmann's work, an example of which is shown on the facing page, decorative inlays in a

mock-dentil pattern establish a strong visual rhythm; dashed inlays in a chevron pattern give the contemporary chests the same effect. The legs of Ruhlmann's chest are positioned to the outside of the carcase, and are defined at the top with an interesting form and at the bottom with an outward flare and a foot of another material. These features are echoed in the contemporary chests.

The chests on the facing page, by John Everdell of Cambridge, Mass., echo the visual rhythms of Art Deco designer Jacques-Emile Ruhlmann's furniture. (Photo by Suzie Cushner.) Below, a cabinet made by Ruhlmann in 1926. (Photo courtesy Alastair Dunkin, Christie's, New York, N.Y.)

In the previous example, the research was based on the work of a particular designer. Research can also be influenced by a technical process (such as bending plywood), function (which involves analysis of a person's physical and emotional requirements for a piece) or a specific object (such as a type of furniture). One of my students recently chose to research daybeds and found that historically the daybed was intended for use in a living area by a severely ill person, so he or she would not have to be confined to the bedroom and isolated from the rest of the family. The student based some of his daybed's concept on this knowledge. As shown in the photo below, grey and black colors represent the ominous state of impending death; glass balls riding in a track in the bed rail give the invalid something with which to while away the remaining hours. A Post-Modern style, which incorporates classical forms derived from architecture (in particular, the stepped forms of the daybed's end sections), marks the piece as something from the 1980s.

Another way research can help generate a concept is by revealing the specific requirements of a particular object. Suppose a furniture maker researched upholstered furniture and discovered a difference between the upholstered chairs used in warm and cold climates. In warm areas, there was much less padding in comparison to the overstuffed furniture found in colder climates. It would be only a small step from this realization to the concept of using upholstery flaps or covers to warm the chair's occupant. This concept could dictate strong new forms for a chair or modification of a conventional chair, as shown in the drawing on the facing page. The designer would have to decide how to develop the concept according to ergonomics, economics and other pertinent information.

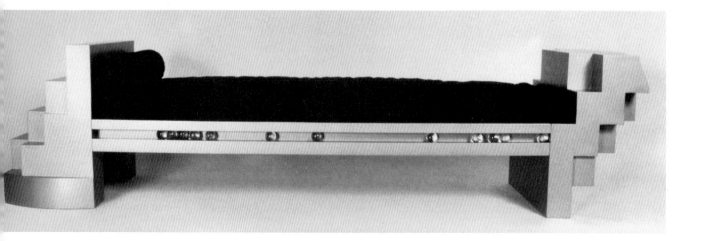

TWO CONCEPTUAL SKETCHES OF AN UPHOLSTERED CHAIR

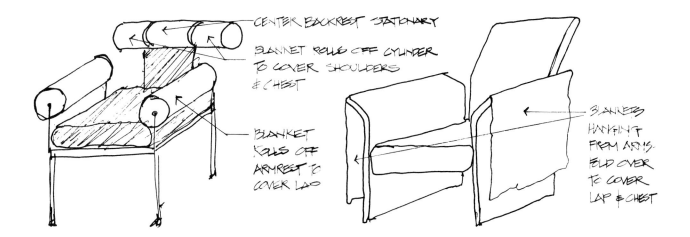

In addition to helping generate a furniture concept, as discussed above, research can be used to refine a concept. But whether I do research before developing a concept or afterward to refine it, I always include a research stage, however brief, in my personal design process. I recommend that beginning designers do likewise. It is always time well spent. Take the instance of a client asking a designer to create a dining-room table. Research might start with such tangible tasks as determining table height in relation to the chairs to be used and the body size of the owners and determining the length, width and general proportions of the table in relation to the room and its traffic patterns. Then the designer would investigate the needs of the clients. Should the table be expandable? Are there any preferences in wood or for other materials? Are there stylistic requirements? Research would also include the designer's observations on appropriate table shape and

FACING PAGE: This daybed by Eric Wolf of New York, N.Y., was designed on the basis of historical research. The piece is made of lacquered birch plywood. Glass balls in the bedrail can be rolled back and forth, providing diversion for the invalid during the course of the illness. (Photo by Gary Gilbert.)

RIGHT: In the dining set by David Powell of Easthampton, Mass., research into the room and the client's requirements refined the concept. As a result, the furniture addresses the needs of the client in a specific functional as well as stylistic sense. (Photo by David Ryan.)

the style that would best complement other furniture in the room. You can see the kind of useful information to be derived.

If a chair concept were based on folding, research might include a review of historical and contemporary folding chairs and of adjustment and folding mechanisms. Other mechanical devices besides those used for chairs—for tripods, for example, or for rulers, easels, pocketknives, car jacks, ski bindings, scaffolding, extension ladders, backpacking tents, cranes and corkscrews—could inspire new ideas on folding or collapsing. During research, the designer would be thinking, "How can I change this, adapt this, make it better or combine this with another idea?" Materials might then be researched as well as technical processes.

The folding chair shown here was designed by one of my students in a class on folding and slotted furniture. The student used research to refine his concept of creating an innovative method of folding while using sheet materials efficiently. The student began his explorations by experimenting with folding cardboard, but through research he learned that mating forms or intricate patterns could be cut out of plywood with a pin (or overarm) router. Research thus inspired the student to change his thinking about cut-out shapes and ways of folding. Subsequent work with cardboard models led to his unique design, in which the chair seat and supports are cut out of the basic frame shape and hinged so they open automatically when the chair is unfolded. The design allows the chair to fold flat to the thickness of two ¾-in. thick pieces of plywood, and there is a minimum amount of waste; three chairs can be cut from a 5x5 sheet of Baltic birch plywood.

research through analysis

I find that sometimes I can gain a great deal of information about a piece of furniture I am designing by consciously analyzing it and writing down my observations. I call this "research through analysis." It is another way of refining a concept. I break down the structure into component parts and think about what each part is, what its limitations are and how it functions within the whole. I analyze the properties of the materials needed. I then analyze the overall

This folding chair by Tom Hamilton of Cranston, R.I., is made of Baltic birch plywood and opens automatically when the chair is unfolded. (Photo by Seth Stem.)

A LAUNDRY HAMPER

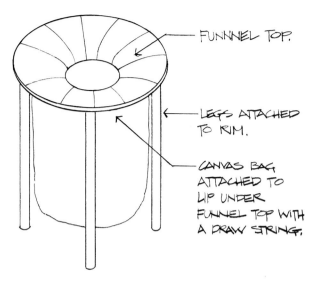

FUNNNEL TOP.

LEGS ATTACHED TO RIM.

CANVAS BAG ATTACHED TO LIP UNDER FUNNEL TOP WITH A DRAW STRING.

function of the piece, and finally how the user interacts with it. This process works especially well with specialized objects. If I were to design a laundry hamper, for example, I could break down the typical hamper into its physical parts:

1. A container of about 2 cu. ft. to 3 cu. ft.;
2. Legs to elevate the container off the floor;
3. A lid to conceal the contents of the hamper;
4. A handle to open the lid;
5. Material that can be wiped clean and will not catch on clothes or deteriorate from moisture.

I would then look at the functional aspects:

1. The lid needs to open from the top or sides;
2. The opening is at least 144 sq. in. and typically about 200 sq. in.;
3. The height of the container is usually 30 in. to 36 in.;
4. The container needs to allow for ventilation.

Then I'd review the questions of how the user would interact with the piece and how the piece would be used.

A man walks into the room with soiled clothes in both hands. He walks over to the hamper, transfers the clothes to the left hand so he can open the lid of the hamper with the right hand. He bends over slightly, opens the lid and holds it open with the right hand at a 45° to 60° angle while depositing the clothes into the hamper with the left hand. The released lid slams shut. The man turns and walks out of the room.

When the hamper is full and it's laundry day, the man walks into the room with an empty clothes basket, bends over to set the basket on the floor in front of the hamper, straightens up partially, lifts the lid with the right hand, holds the lid open with the left hand, lifts some of the soiled clothes out of the hamper with the right hand and puts them into the basket. He repeats this motion until the hamper is empty, each time bending farther down from the waist to reach the clothes at the bottom. The hamper lid is released and drops down. The man bends over and picks up the clothes basket with both hands, and turns to walk to the laundry room. On the way to the laundry room is an interior door, which is closed. The man balances the clothes basket on his hip with the left hand so that he can open the door with the right hand.

If you didn't write them down, you might not recognize how many motions there really are in using a typical hamper. Analysis of the user's movement suggests some waste while walking to and from the hamper, an awkward series of physical movements while opening the hamper lid and holding onto clothes, and excessive bending and motion in transferring the clothes from the hamper to the clothes basket when the clothes are to be washed. To address some of the waste and awkwardness, I might design a laundry hamper such as the one on the facing page, which eliminates the need for the clothes basket. The top is funnel-shaped so clothes can be tossed in (from several feet away, if need be) without lifting a lid. A canvas bag attached to the lid under the funnel top with a drawstring may be removed and taken directly to the laundry room. Much of the innovation here comes from ergonomic analysis—the simple study of user interaction with an object.

the process of innovation

The level of innovation you bring to a concept can depend on how you define the design problem. Consider the vacuum cleaner. When everybody used brooms, the design problem was always to make a better broom—be it wider, or made of stiffer materials, or shaped to reach into corners and crevices. The concept of the vacuum cleaner did not develop until somebody realized that the broom wasn't the problem, the *dirt* was. In the case of furniture, if you wanted to design an innovative chair, the first thing you would have to do is to realize that the problem is not how to design a chair to support people, but how to support people in a resting position. To solve this problem, you would have to broaden the way you think about chairs. One approach is to abstract your thinking—any word that made you think of a specific form, such as "chair," would have to go. Looking at a design problem this way eliminates many preconceived notions. Instead you have to think of things that are at the root of what you are trying to do.

The design of this dining chair by Greg Draudt of Cambridge, Mass., was the result of a fairly simple analysis of user interaction. The way most people hike their chairs forward when sitting down at a table inspired the idea of using wheels at the front to help the chair roll forward. (Photo by Seth Stem.)

The rocking chair on the facing page is a product of this method of thinking. For the concept of this chair I initially removed the word "rocking" from the design problem and concentrated on the word "movement," which could imply swinging, gliding, rolling, pivoting, skating and turning as well as rocking. I finally came up with a combination of rocking and pivoting movements, so the chair rocks from side to side instead of from front to back. If I had confined my thinking to conventional rockers, I probably wouldn't have broken out of the conventional rocking-chair format.

Throughout the process of design, it's sometimes difficult to comprehend the impact or importance of an idea. I see this often with my students when we review sketchbooks—many of my students question the validity of their ideas and, in their search for the perfect solution, tend to overlook some good ideas they've already sketched out. So I stress that it's important to develop the ability to recognize worthwhile ideas when trying to create a new piece of furniture. There's no way to teach somebody how to do this; in many cases it's simply a matter of developing self-confidence. A designer is like the songwriter who, in plotting the first notes to a song, can recognize their strength and meaning and project onto them the effect of varied instrumentation, tone, volume dynamics and verse. In the same way, a furniture designer must learn to recognize a good idea or a visually promising piece from a rough sketch, develop the essence of the design, and then embellish it through the use of materials, finishes and details. Unfortunately, there is no way to teach this. Experience is the best instructor.

Seth Stem's rocking chair moves from side to side instead of front to back. (Photo by Gary Gilbert.)

design development

Once you have established a strong concept, the next step is to give the furniture physical shape. It is time to solve the aesthetic, structural and functional problems of the piece, as well as to analyze, investigate and refine the design in the way that best expresses the concept. In other words, it is time to draw, make models and mockups, select materials and construction methods, and settle on details. This process is called design development.

The approach you take to design affects its development, and there are myriad approaches. At one extreme is the philosophy of designing from technical information, that is, working within the parameters of a particular technique or group of tech-

BELOW: The process of edge-gluing beveled wood pieces into ribbonlike shapes dictates the strong form of this table by Peter Michael Adams of Hobart, Tasmania, Australia. (Photo by Dan Bailey.)

FACING PAGE: The fluid grace of this small bedside table by David Rogers of Lynchburg, Va., also results from the edge-gluing process. (Photo by David Rogers.)

niques. While this does not necessarily produce static designs, it can influence the look of a piece by limiting the types of forms allowed to evolve. For example, the pieces shown here were both constructed with edge-glued beveled members, and while both pieces have strong, dynamic forms, you can tell the designs were dictated by the technique.

At the other extreme is the philosophy of creating the design and then figuring out how to make it. Designing on the basis of form allows a broader range of design options, but a greater number of technical

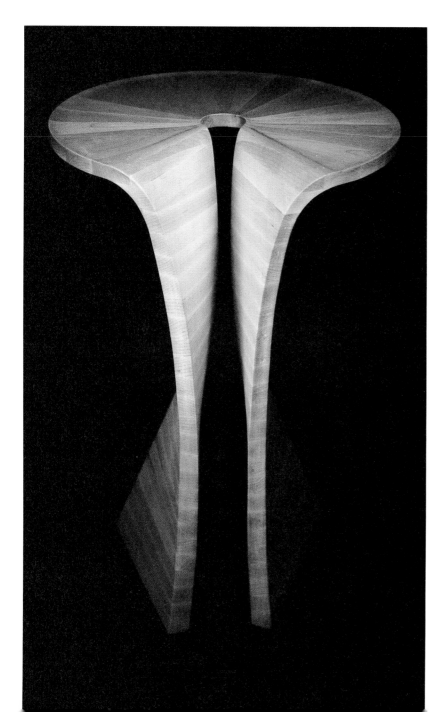

problems can arise, and in many cases the form or details eventually have to be compromised during construction. For example, the bold geometric forms of the veneered chair on the facing page were designed with unusually thick parts. The designer, who was unfamiliar with furniture-making techniques, relied on the people who developed the prototype to figure out construction methods. The chair gained great recognition as a Post-Modern piece, but it is expensive to produce because of the bent-plywood core and veneering involved. Also, the veneered surfaces leave exposed edges that are quite vulnerable to damage.

I find it's easiest to design when I temporarily divorce myself from the thought that "I'm going to have to build this thing." But although I'm a strong advocate of designing on the basis of form, I also design from technical information when appropriate, especially if I've become excited about a new material or process. Naturally, the more you know about technique, materials and technology, the more successfully you can develop a form-based design into a final piece of furniture.

eight design steps

Here is a rundown of the steps that I usually go through in developing a design. What follows is a nuts-and-bolts description of procedure from which discusssion of the very heart of design (form, proportion, composition and other elements of what I call the "visual vocabulary") has been deliberately omitted. These elements are explored in detail in the next section of this book. So bear in mind that while you are proceeding through the eight steps on this list, you will also be juggling numerous aesthetic issues.

A note of caution—beginning designers shouldn't be discouraged if they can't deal with everything at once. My first-year design students generally have little or no technical expertise. For their first project, which is usually a table, I have them create a simple form and concentrate mostly on proportion, details and structure. This way they don't get too carried away with conceptual notions that they

The concept of using unusually thick forms for this chair, designed by architect Michael Graves of New York City, evolved completely independently of any consideration of technique. The construction, which is veneer over hardwood and plywood, was worked out while making a prototype. (Photo by Dan Gratiot.)

don't have the technical skills to carry out. Some of my students have to build two or three pieces before they are ready to acquire a more sophisticated visual vocabulary. If you are a beginner, give yourself a similar gentle introduction to design. Also keep in mind that every design problem is different, and therefore the list of steps may vary from situation to situation. Your logic is the best guide to what to include.

step 1: reviewing the problem I usually begin by referring to the problem statement and concept developed during conceptualization, as discussed on pp. 4-7. This statement might be altered, revised or refined as new information is added over the course of the work. A problem statement might read "design a hallway table that will enhance the foyer of the client's contemporary home." The concept could be to build a contemporary, elegant piece that relates to strong architectural elements in the foyer and functions to facilitate the activities of people entering or leaving the house.

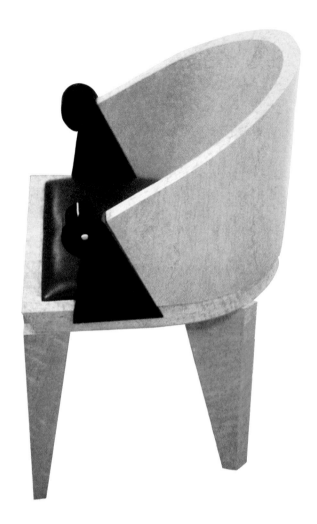

step 2: creating a list of requirements Start by writing down all the requirements of the piece, such as function, dimensions, colors and materials. Much of this information will probably have been generated during the research stage (see pp. 8-15), but now is the time to list additional specifics. I use this data as a guide to resolve practical and aesthetic questions. The idea is to reveal areas of flexibility in the project while progressing in a way that's compatible with the concept. For example, for the hallway table, my list might include:
— the height of the table surface;
— the optimum length and width of the table relative to the size of the entryway;
— the feet of the table must be made of a material that will not scratch the polished stone floor of the entryway;
— the table should incorporate some storage for gloves, scarves, keys and so on;
— the form of the table should blend with the strong forms of the arched-top entrance door;
— the table is to be made of bird's-eye maple, as the client requested.

step 3: selecting visual references and icons After making the list of requirements for the piece of furniture, I usually quickly sketch out the various forms the concept might take. If inspiration is lacking, I will give some thought at this time to adopting a visual reference or icon (pp. 34-40), which might help to generate some new ideas and to tie the piece together aesthetically.

step 4: form generation Another process I sometimes use in design if no visual inspiration arises is that of form generation. I might or might not have a predetermined shape in mind, but by going through this process it is always possible to generate more options. Some options will be useful, some just strange, but almost certainly forms will evolve that would otherwise go undiscovered. In some pieces, the forms can be modified to integrate function; in others they can be used as details. Some projects lend themselves to this process better than others. The forms generated for a jewelry box, for instance, could be usable as well as exciting because a jewelry box can still function well even if it deviates from the standard notion of "box." Conversely, the form-generation process might not be as useful in the design of a dining chair, where dimensions and angles of seating surfaces are rigidly fixed.

For best results, approach this process with as few preconceived ideas as possible. This way, you won't rule out exciting ideas because of initial constraints.

FACING PAGE, TOP LEFT: A two-dimensional shape translated into a three-dimensional wood or Styrofoam model sometimes yields a form that has direct application to a piece of furniture. The one in the photo, for example, could be used as a table leg. (Photo by Seth Stem.)

FACING PAGE, TOP RIGHT: The second set of images is drawn upon the original model. (Photo by Seth Stem.)

FACING PAGE, BOTTOM: Here are the final forms for the hallway table. (Photo by Seth Stem.)

SOME SHAPES FOR A FORM-GENERATION EXERCISE (HALLWAY TABLE)

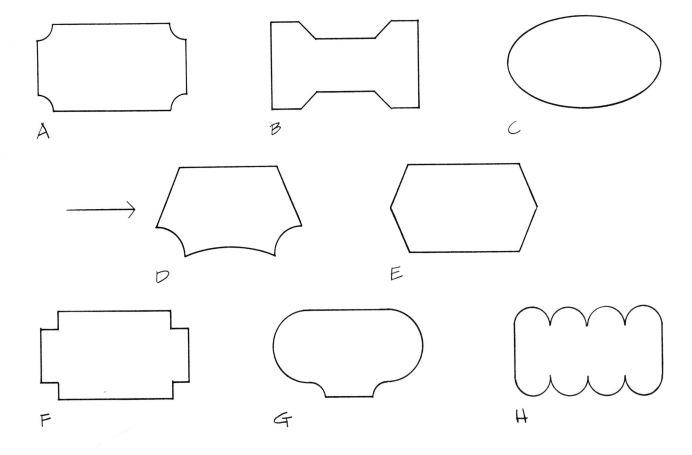

The first step in form generation is to create a number of two-dimensional images in plan view. Randomly or rationally select the images—be loose and you will get radical results; be conservative and you will end up with more usable information, but maybe nothing inspired. The more you limit yourself to obvious forms, the more preconceived notions you'll impose on the project.

The drawing on the facing page contains some possible images for the hallway table described in the problem statement and concept. In this case, we'll be following the development of "D."

The second step is to make the image into a three-dimensional object, in a small scale if necessary, out of wood, Styrofoam or any other material, as shown in the photo at near right. At this point, the three-dimensional form may already be usable as part of a piece, for example, as a table leg.

The third step is to superimpose a variety of new two-dimensional images on one side of the three-dimensional form, as shown in the photo at far right. These images again may be representational (a star, gear or butterfly) or abstract, or relate to the function of a piece of furniture.

The fourth step is to cut out the superimposed images on the three-dimensional form to produce new three-dimensional shapes, as shown in the photo below. These are then used as the form for the whole piece or for a detail—perhaps a handle or foot treatment. If you push this process, you will

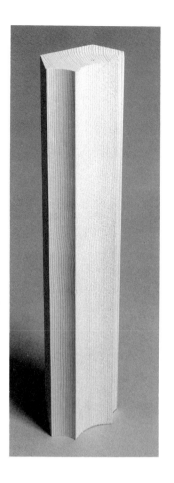

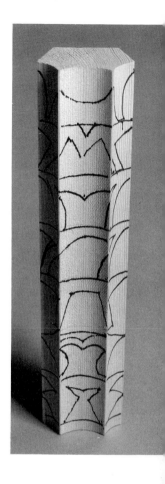

probably achieve complex forms that you would have had a hard time imagining. Feel free to reorient the forms upside down and sideways. Remember, this exercise is to develop options. Reoriented pieces may inspire a different use—for example, a part of the form might lend itself to a lip or a handle when viewed vertically, but no such application is suggested horizontally. The legs and stretchers of the table below were generated using steps 1 and 2 of this form-generation process.

step 5: the option review When I was just starting out in my design career, a former employer

Turning a two-dimensional shape into a three-dimensional one, as shown in the photos on p. 23, resulted in this table, by Scott Willens of Providence, R.I. Both the legs and apron rails were developed this way. (Photo by Scott Willens.)

gave me some advice that has proved invaluable. She told me to evaluate all the possible options when making a design, choose the best approach, immediately assume that I had made the wrong choice, and then proceed. With this attitude, she explained, it would be impossible to make an irrevocable decision. The door would remain open to evaluation and improvement throughout the design and construction of the piece. Over the years, I have come to believe that reviewing a good array of options is critical to unearthing the best solutions to the functional, structural and aesthetic requirements of furniture. Given more thought, just about any design can be improved. So I always make it a practice to put each project through this review before making the working drawings.

The drawings on pp. 25-29 show how I might review just one design detail—a stretcher in the hallway table. You choose among the options by weighing their appropriateness to the concept and by using good aesthetic judgment, as outlined in the next section of this book.

reversing   As shown in the drawing below, reversing consists of experimenting with recessed and

SOME OPTIONS FOR A HALLWAY-TABLE STRETCHER: REVERSING

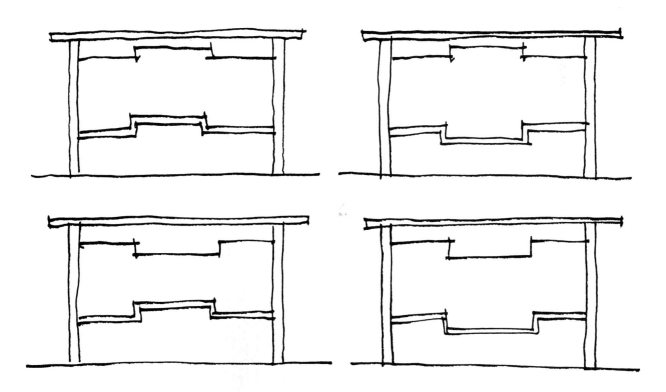

protruding forms. In a chest with a drawer, try moving the drawer from the bottom to the top or from one side to the other. Turning a table base upside down can generate new possibilities.

changing size/scale Manipulating the size of the stretcher radically changes its character. Doubling the size of the legs would have the same effect.

reviewing materials Evaluate materials for strength, stability and durability. A chair with a cantilevered seat might be more stable if aluminum were used instead of wood. An extremely delicate, lightweight chair designed in bent wood might be stronger if made from carbon fiber.

experimenting with parts Try more parts, fewer parts, hidden parts, exposed parts, integrated parts. See what the piece looks like with three stretchers instead of one.

increasing/decreasing complexity Develop a strong ornamental quality in the details of a piece, or strip it down to its essence. Consider adding pat-

CHANGING SIZE/SCALE

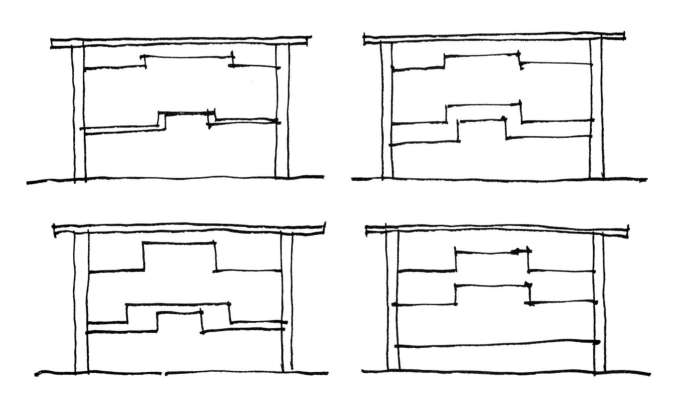

EXPERIMENTING WITH PARTS

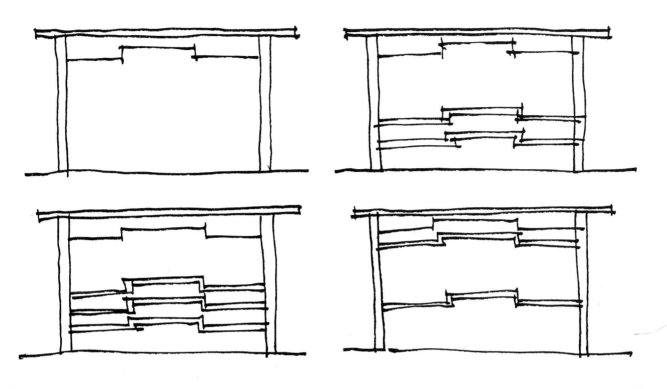

INCREASING/DECREASING COMPLEXITY

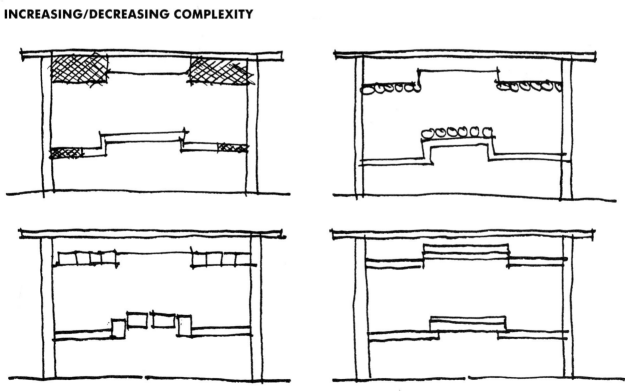

MANIPULATING SYMPATHETIC AND CONTRASTING FORMS

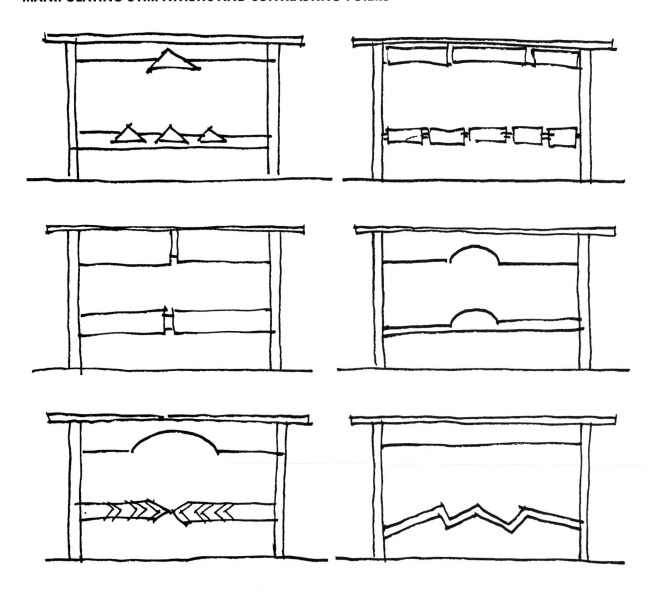

ADDING CLARITY/VAGUENESS

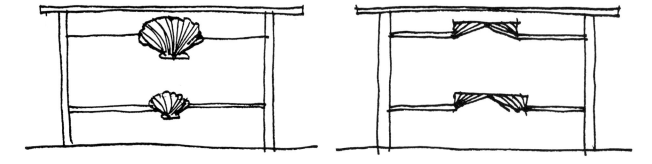

tern or texture to all the surfaces or to part of one. Use a direct solution to a hinging problem or make the hinge so complex that it becomes a strong visual element in itself.

manipulating sympathetic and contrasting forms
In the case of the hallway table, experiment with geometric or organic forms. In a bed, transfer the flowing curvilinear forms of the headboard to the rail. For variety, you might try to create a chair with a circular back, rectangular seat and triangular details. Use subdued or flamboyant forms, which are sympathetic or contrasting.

adding clarity/vagueness For the stretcher, create a representational image or an abstract version of the same image, introducing non-pictorial qualities of animation or form.

adjusting placement Move the stretcher as low or high as possible. Try the handle of a door along the edge and in the center. Place a carved detail in an obvious place on the outside of a door or on the inside for a surprise.

ADJUSTING PLACEMENT

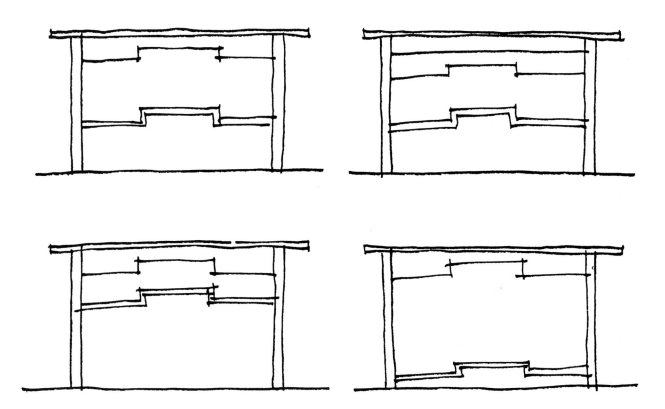

Numerous options, two of which are shown in the drawings below, were considered before the final design for the chair shown on the facing page was determined. (See the mockups on pp. 189-190.) The concept was to allow the sitter to assume a variety of positions in one chair. The final prototype had a high right side and low, extended left arm, to permit the user to sit frontways or sideways, as if in a lounge chair. The left extension provides a leg rest.

A number of options and variations of form and function were considered in drawings (shown on the facing page) and mockups (shown on pp. 189-190) for this chair by Bill Wurz of San Francisco, Calif. (Photo by Gary Gilbert.)

step 6: the materials review When I finally have a sketch of a form that expresses the concept of the piece, I begin to think about materials. The search for materials centers on choosing the most appropriate—finding wood of the right density, color or flexibility or finding a material with high strength, such as alloy steel. Be sure to check out the availability of materials and hardware. There's nothing worse than starting construction and finding out that the hinges you want are back-ordered and won't be in for another three months, or that the 14-ft. stainless-steel rod you need comes only in 12-ft. lengths. Cost is another important factor. I once had a student who designed a chair that included some large-diameter acrylic cylinders. Partway into construction he found that the cost of the acrylic for the job would be $3,000. He quickly changed his design.

Materials are closely linked to the technical processes that will be used to build the piece, so you really can't look at one without the other. For instance, the curved forms of a coffee table under design might be conceived as bent-plywood elements with veneered surfaces, but they also could be made in sheet brass, cast from vatican stone or made from vacuum-formed plastic.

step 7: the feasibility review At this time you look at how practical the design is in terms of structural integrity, durability and function (and marketing and manufacturing, if applicable). Make prototypes and evaluate costs. For example, if your client wants a rosewood dining table and the materials budget is $200, the project is probably not feasible.

The mirror at left, which was to be a production item, is an example of a project that failed the feasibility review. The outside frame was constructed from a piece of aluminum flatstock, bent at the corners and butt-welded where the ends of the stock met. Inside the aluminum frame was a wood frame, and quartered sections of a wood turning decorated the outside. The design had merit in that the combi-

ABOVE LEFT: The prototype for this mirror designed by Jon Benson of Providence, R.I., revealed a tolerance problem in fitting the wood frame into the surrounding aluminum frame. (Photo by Seth Stem.)

FACING PAGE: Design options for a chair were quickly reviewed by doing a series of scale models in Styrofoam, foamcore and plastic rod in a collaborative effort by William Bellows and Fred Spector of Providence, R.I. (Photo by Seth Stem.)

nation of materials was interesting and the processes used to produce the turned forms were efficient. But the prototype revealed a problem fitting the wood frame into the aluminum frame. Each side of the aluminum frame bowed when its corners were bent, and the welding created slight variations in size. The wood frame therefore had to be hand-planed and filed to fit, and this time-consuming task substantially raised the cost of the mirror.

step 8: models, working drawings, mockups

After sketching and deciding on the options, the design is pretty well established. Next I'll often make a scale model, like the ones in the photo below, so

that what I've drawn can be seen in three dimensions and checked for flaws. Full-scale (whenever possible) preliminary working drawings are next. These help the designer assess the proportions of the piece and decide on details. It is very important that these drawings be in true scale so that the judgments based on them will be accurate.

Making one or several mockups is the next step. Mockups are full-size representations of part of the design or of the entire piece. Making a mockup of each detail you're unsure of will help you refine its line, mass, detail, function and connections. Revise the working drawings after the mockup stage. Working drawings, scale models and mockups are discussed in detail in the appendices (pp. 164-191).

visual references and icons

When the aesthetics of a piece do not seem to come together naturally, it is often worthwhile to develop a visual reference or icon to aid in design. These are widely used in industrial design to give strong direction to an object and to avoid visual clutter. Basically, using something as a visual reference entails ana-

lyzing its essence and then transferring it (or one or several interesting elements) to the design in progress. Using something as an icon means viewing it in terms of its cultural or stylistic symbolism. For example, if you were to use a Coca-Cola can as a visual reference, you could incorporate into a furniture piece the can's metallic red color or its cylindrical shape. If you used the can as an icon, you would then incorporate the intangible elements of the product's image, perhaps by designing a youthful or exuberant feel into the piece.

As another example, consider the photo on the facing page. You could use any of the drinks as a visual reference in about the same way. Interesting elements of the ice-cream soda might be the bent straw, the shape of the glass and the color of the ice cream. In the gin-and-tonic, the effervescence and the radiating lines in the lime slice and the way it intersects the rim of the glass are appealing. Useful components of the martini would be the slick glass surface, the way the main volume of the glass is supported by a thin stem, the swizzle stick and the color contrast between the stick and the olive.

Any of these elements could guide a furniture design. For example, the soda straw could inspire a chair leg that reflects the straw's shape. Or it could affect the look of the piping on an upholstered seat. Perhaps the entire furniture surface could be modeled on the slick, glossy image of the martini glass.

If we were to use the drinks as icons, the exercise would work quite differently, because the drinks would be valued for the associations they generate as symbols of culture or style. Like the soda can, the ice-cream soda represents youth and energy, the corner drugstore, bright colors and fun. The gin-and-tonic hints at leisure—sunny days at beach or poolside. The martini suggests elegance, black ties and nightclubs. Any of these associations could be used to help direct the design of a piece. If the piece were a chair, for example, a designer using these drinks as icons might come up with one that fits the lifestyles and fads of a teenager, one to be used in leisure and relaxation, and one that is geared to a formal environment. When several icons are used at

FACING PAGE: Each drink shown here—an ice-cream soda, a gin-and-tonic and a martini—suggests different visual references and icons. (Photo by Seth Stem.)

RIGHT: This chest by Wendy Maruyama of Oakland, Calif., used the highboy and classical architecture as visual references. (Photo by Bob Robinson.)

the same time, the results can be striking, as the example at left illustrates.

A visual reference or icon can be developed while conceptualizing or researching a design, or during the design-development stage (pp. 20-34). To use a visual reference or an icon, you simply select a non-furniture object, extract its essence (or "personality") and apply this to the looks or mechanics of the piece, either literally or abstractly. In the case of a visual reference, the essence can relate to whatever quality you think is important, be it form, color, material, pattern, transitions between parts, texture or mechanical workings. As with a concept, once you have established a visual reference or icon, consult it each time a visual problem or question occurs in the evolution of the design. Sometimes the concept of a piece and its visual reference or icon will be inseparable; sometimes the visual reference or icon will be overlaid onto the concept. For example, a designer could base the concept for a folding chair on a new hinging device, and the aesthetics on the beautiful forms and polished surfaces of the fenders and engine castings of a BMW motorcycle—this chair would have a sleek, sophisticated feel. But if a clown were chosen for the reference, the chair would have quite a different look, perhaps derived from images of painted faces, colorful costumes and balloons. It's important to understand, however, that the visual reference is intended to help the designer make critical design decisions. It needn't be translated so literally in the piece that it is identifiable to the viewer, although of course it can be. Contrast the Sottsass cabinet at left to the literal reference of the chair on the facing page.

LEFT: Casablanca Cabinet by Ettore Sottsass of Milan, Italy (Memphis, 1981), was suggested by a mix of icons—science fiction, graffiti, Jackson Pollock paintings and the architecture of Le Corbusier. The cabinet isn't easy to associate with any one of these; rather, the icons bring a unique aesthetic to the piece. (Photo by Aldo Ballo.)

FACING PAGE, LEFT: All American Make-Up Mirror dressing table by Paul Sasso of Murray, Ky., used carnivals and fairs for its icons and so it has a lively, festive air. (Photo by Paul Sasso.)

FACING PAGE, RIGHT: The Roadrunner cartoon character was used as a visual reference to develop the personality and humor in this chair by Mark Hazel of Providence, R.I. The concept was to do a chair series using a wire framework for structure and to develop the character of each chair by assigning it a familiar image. (Photo by Seth Stem.)

The chairs shown in the photo below could probably have profited from the conscious use of a visual reference or icon to unify their design. The concept was to make several knock-down chairs from the same bent-plywood shape, each having a different character. The blue chair, which uses a large nylon barrel nut for assembly, works well because its color, form and materials combine to create unity, and the exposed hardware tells how the chair is built. In the yellow chair, which was developed next, the designer took a no-tool-in-assembly approach, which resulted in a cylindrical form in the base that allowed access for hand-tightened hardware. But the understructure, which has a slightly mechanical feel, doesn't relate strongly to the back and seat, the character of which was derived from a historical shield chair. In the red chair, the cylindrical form for the hardware connection was enlarged for better access. This chair is more completely resolved than its yellow predecessor, because the circular form in the base complements the shapes in the back, seat and legs. However, both the red and yellow chairs still feel somewhat eclectic, and I would argue that had the designer consciously selected a visual reference for each and carried out its essence in form, detailing and color, the chairs would have made a much stronger statement.

Sometimes a designer's previous work becomes a strong visual reference that dictates the style of all subsequent projects. When I first started to design and make furniture, I just assumed everybody had a natural style within which he or she should work. It

BELOW: These three chairs in a series by Chris Freed of Providence, R.I., all use the same bent-plywood shape in profile, but have completely different characters. (Photo by Seth Stem.)

FACING PAGE: The forms of Seth Stem's jewelry cabinet and floor mirror are based on bent-lamination techniques. (Photo of jewelry cabinet by Gary Gilbert; photo of floor mirror by Marc Harrison.)

never occurred to me that I could consciously manipulate the aesthetic of my work. Because my early pieces focused on bent laminated wood, I continued to explore compound-curved forms in conjunction with controlled symmetrical shapes. The two pieces shown in the photos below are typical of my work in the late 1970s. Their style emerged from technique and from my concern with strong forms and flowing transitions between parts. As my work progressed, I realized all the pieces looked more or less the same, and I began to see just how limited my approach was. For some projects I wasn't even looking for an appropriate aesthetic, style or material—I was simply using what I was comfortable with. There is nothing wrong with doing this, and many

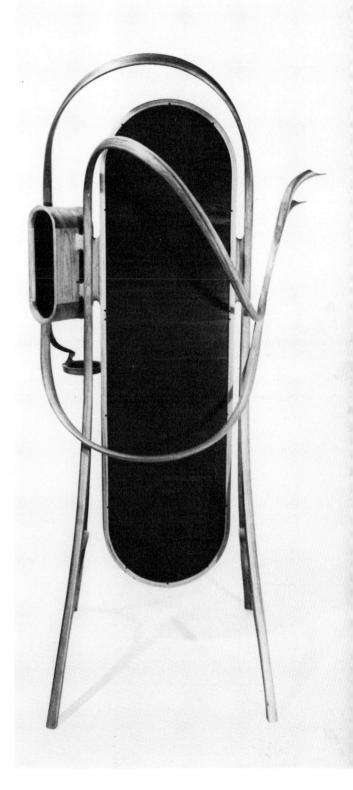

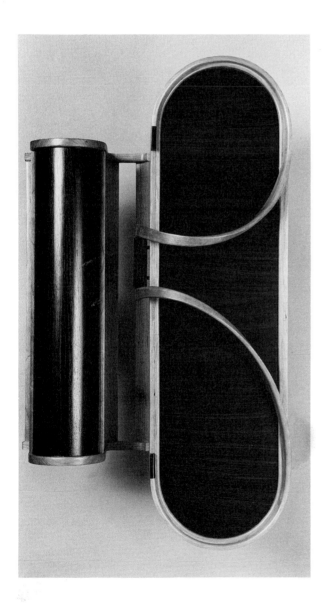

furniture makers have gained great recognition working just this way. Still, I realized it wasn't the only approach.

I then decided to use non-furniture objects as visual references. An example of the results is shown on the facing page. The concept was to contrast a rough, massive material and form with delicate, precious elements. The visual references I chose were architectural buttresses in concrete to suggest mass, and elaborate jewelry with repetitive faceted gems held in delicate mounts to suggest preciousness. The result of using visual references was not so much an advancement in my creativity as an increase in my freedom to develop diversified styles and in my control of the visual information my work conveyed. Also, the search for a reference is fun, because of the possibilities of form, color, texture and materials that can develop.

building and evaluating the design

A comprehensive discussion of the construction issues inherent in making furniture would fill several books. On this topic I'll note here only that it's safest and most efficient to resolve all the design issues of a piece of furniture before construction begins. Naturally, it's valuable to see the work in a model, too. Few designers work that way, however. Instead, they re-evaluate design and detailing and make improvements as they go. For me, absolute understanding of a piece develops only when I see it three dimensionally in full scale and with real materials.

In addition, when a designer makes one-of-a-kind pieces, the chance to revise or fine-tune a piece in its second generation is rare, and perhaps even undesirable for those who feel little personal satisfaction in making the piece twice. I think continual design evaluation throughout construction is essential to obtaining the best results. This means stepping back now and then and looking at the work with a critical eye.

Once a piece is done, set aside some time to evaluate it. Look at its successes and failures, what you like and dislike, what you would do again and what you would change if you were to do it over. You can do this critique by yourself to some extent,

The form, materials and details in Seth Stem's table (facing page) developed through the use of gems (above left) and architectural buttresses as visual references. (Gem photo by Seth Stem; table photo by Gary Gilbert.)

but usually it's good to invite others to comment on your work. In this way you will gain a fresh perspective on what others see in the piece. Try to separate substantive and objective comments from those based purely on taste. It is far more helpful to hear that the form of your piece is disliked because the balance of the mass to the right is not adequately offset by the three rails on the left than simply to hear, "I don't like the way it looks." Try to get at the reasons behind such subjective criticisms. Ask questions like "Why don't you like the way it looks?" or "Just why do you feel it is uncomfortable—is it hitting your back the wrong way?"

It helps to find a compatible woodworker or furniture designer and make an agreement to critique each other's work. It also helps to have your work reviewed by a non-woodworker who is involved in art or design in some other capacity. A person like this is less likely to get caught up in the technical questions and will be more apt to respond to the formal design issues.

When I work on a complex project for a long time—say six to eight weeks—I have a hard time evaluating it accurately, especially just after finishing it. I get too caught up in details, mistakes I might have made that really bother me, and I am not able to admit to myself, after all that work, that there might have been a better or an easier solution. After a few weeks to six months, I can usually set aside the emotional aspects of designing and making and give my own work a clear and lucid evaluation.

presenting the design

Educating clients about the amount of thought, effort and creativity that goes into your furniture will help build your reputation and sell your work. My

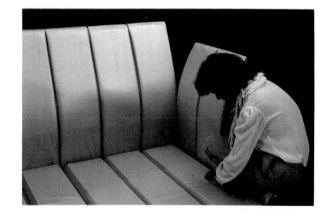

clients like to see a record of my work processes—
the quantity, quality, consistency and diversity of
what I've done. They particularly appreciate a slide
show of the design and construction processes involved in making a piece. A slide show of the piece
itself can also be extremely important. The photo
sequence shown here illustrates the transportability,
assembly, comfort and use of a knock-down couch.
A live demonstration of these features would be less
effective because of the time required to assemble
parts and hardware.

Photos of finished work in both black-and-white
and color are especially important, even if you're
not selling the piece, because you can control lighting and background and present the piece from its
best angle. Good slides add a level of professional-
ism to the work and often enhance its appearance,
too. Slides are valuable for publicity purposes. The
opportunity may arise to publish your work in a
newspaper, magazine or book.

As a general procedure, it's a good idea to keep on
hand several 8x10 black-and-white prints and some
color transparencies of your favorite or most recent
work. Slides are all right, but larger transparencies
are desirable; the larger the format, the better the
quality of the reproduction. If you have your work
photographed professionally, ask to have a 4x5 or at
least a medium-format (2¼ in. square) transparency
made. Color reproductions for publication are usually done from a transparency, and color prints can
also be made from them.

**The assembly and use of this transportable couch by
Sheila Danko of Ithaca, N.Y., are well illustrated in a
slide presentation. (Photos by Sheila Danko.)**

A VISUAL VOCABULARY

A designer creates a piece of furniture by manipulating any combination of elements chosen from a vast menu of design possibilities. I call this menu the "visual vocabulary." Just as the vocabulary of words we know shapes the way we speak, a full vocabulary of design elements gives a designer the means to express ideas clearly and eloquently in three-dimensional form.

The elements of the visual vocabulary fall into three groups. The first is form. Factors that affect form are line weight (the visual width of a part or element), positive/negative space and animation, among others. The second group consists of composition and proportion. Composition is the arrangement of forms within an object or the arrangement of elements within a form; proportion is the spatial relationship of parts to each other and to the whole. The third group is color and surface treatment, encompassing texture and ornamentation.

Although each group is discussed in a separate chapter in this section, design is not necessarily a linear process. Far from it. From the very first sketches, a design is likely to consider proportion, composition and color, among other factors, simultaneously.

A visual vocabulary develops differently for everyone. Some designers experiment constantly, selecting a different palette of elements for every piece. Consider the cabinet at top right on p. 46. Its designer, Garry Knox Bennett, is known for his use of bold forms and vivid colors. Yet this piece is a model of restraint and refinement (except for the nail in the side). Here Bennett deliberately stepped out of his idiom and consciously selected the elements that would best support his concept (which concerns the trend toward hyperpreciousness in contemporary furniture). A nail driven into the side of one of Bennett's typical pieces (see p. 140), would hardly have the same effect.

Success is also possible, however, within a more circumscribed vocabulary. Sam Maloof's work, for example, is characterized by sculpted seats, swelling joints, natural wood colors and flowing transitions. Typically, intersecting frame parts don't end abruptly—armrests overhang the front legs, for instance, and back legs extend above the crest rail, as in the rocking chair on p. 46. Each piece, though executed in the same style, is lively and distinct.

Just as there's no best way to develop a visual vocabulary, there are no rigid rules for using elements within it. But keep the following three guidelines in mind as you design:

Choosing to work with
a visual vocabulary
consisting of precise forms
and fine detailing resulted
in a very controlled,
elegant piece.
This Lady's Writing Desk
was designed and made
by Peter Spadone
of Kennebunk, Maine.
(Photo by Peter Spadone.)

TOP LEFT: The detailing of these two cedar chests by Jack Larimore of Philadelphia, Pa., reads very differently in painted and natural versions. (Photos by Rick Echelmeyer.)

TOP RIGHT: Nail Cabinet by Garry Knox Bennett of Oakland, Calif. The refined appearance of this piece contrasts with the effect of the nail driven into its side, a comment on hyperpreciousness in furniture. (Photos by Garry Knox Bennett.)

ABOVE: Sam Maloof's recognizable style, evident in this rocking chair, includes sculpted seats and swelling joints. Maloof, of Alta Loma, Calif., also uses monochromatic wood colors. (Photo by Moore, Ontario, Calif.)

1. Support the concept visually. To avoid getting lost in the maze of possibilities, stick closely to your concept (see pp. 4-7). Determine the main issues, and then edit the visual information accordingly. For example, if the intent is to make a piece appear massive, concentrate on form and proportion. Use other elements, such as texture, to support the concept. But beware of sabotaging yourself by adding inappropriate detail.

2. Avoid visual confusion. A common tendency is to squeeze in as much visual information as possible—many otherwise successful pieces have been ruined by too much exposed joinery or too many species of wood. (Edge-gluing different species together to produce racing stripes is a common device. Unfortunately, the stripes often don't relate to anything else.)

If you make a point of limiting visual information, you'll realize that some plainly doesn't belong. For example, in the first violin display case in the drawing below, the structure of the door frame interferes with the view of the violin. Also, the exposed through-dovetail joinery is distracting (the violin is on display, not the joinery) and its ostentation clashes with the refined violin. A hidden spline miter would be more appropriate here, as would a one-piece door, perhaps hinged at the top, so the view of the instrument wouldn't be obstructed.

3. Select elements of the visual vocabulary that harmonize with the design. Success here comes from experience and sensitivity, and again, from a clear concept. Materials have unique characteristics that enhance or detract from the overall design. Look at the cedar chests on the facing page. The painted surface of the chest at top allows the refined detailing of the piece to be easily read. By contrast, the knots, sapwood and grain of the unpainted cedar chest at bottom conflict with the detailing.

TWO VIOLIN CASES

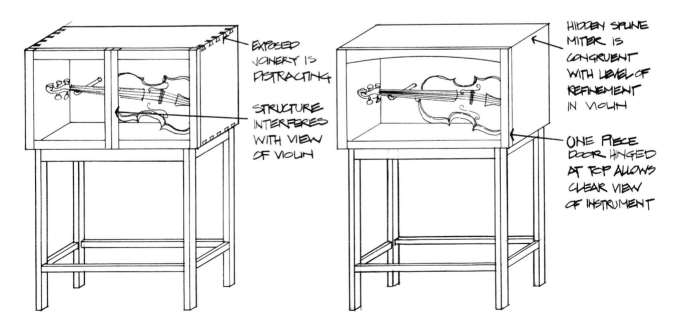

form

Form is the perceived geometry of the volume and mass of an object. It is often the thing we notice first in furniture. All furniture has some sort of form, even if it appears relatively shapeless.

The form of a piece of furniture should provide three levels of information. The first lets the viewer recognize the piece as a chair, table or whatever. More subtly, form can also distinguish objects that look similar but have different functions—for instance, a viewer might be able to tell a backless bench from a coffee table only because of the slight concave form of the bench top or the delicate form of the coffee table's understructure. Form at this level also establishes overall character—whether the piece is organic, elegant or attention-grabbing.

The second level of form gives visual information on how to interact with a piece. For example, chairs have myriad forms, but all are for sitting; the forms of cabinets suggest storage or display. On this level, form tells the viewer where to open a cabinet door, where to grab an armrest, or how to work an extension table.

The third level of form is more intimate, and concerns fine detailing such as carving, hardware, molding and inlays. This is the level of information that closely holds our interest when we interact with the piece, and prevents boredom with the visual information presented on the first two levels.

Whether natural or manmade, forms are composed primarily of combinations of basic geometric shapes or their variations. Cubes, spheres, cones, pyramids and cylinders can be explored individually or in combination to create a furniture form. Although a form can take shape spontaneously, designers also use formal exercises to develop forms if there is no inspiration (see pp. 22-24).

Too often woodworkers rely on craftsmanship, joinery or materials to carry a design. These matters are important, of course, but no one element should dominate the others. Evaluate form in furniture under design by mentally painting it grey and asking the following questions: Does the form stand by itself? Is it suitable for its intended use? Is it interesting and visually dynamic? Does it achieve these things without material richness and structural or joinery information? If you can answer yes to these questions, then the form has credibility and the design is proceeding in the right direction. Add detail, high-quality craftsmanship, gorgeous materials, color and any other necessary elements to a successful form and a well-designed piece of furniture will almost certainly result.

Designers usually deal with the piece's overall form first, then use detail either to support it or contrast with it. This is not a hard-and-fast rule, however, and many designs are developed by concentrating on details first (see pp. 56-59). But much of what's true about overall form also applies to detail form.

six principles of overall form

The designer has an incredible amount of latitude in creating a furniture form, even when the piece has to fulfill a narrow function. For example, a dining-room table traditionally has a flat surface atop an understructure arranged to accommodate the diners' feet and legs. Once these requirements have been met, there are still many options. The table base may have four legs or be a trestle or central pedestal. Each of these options could be executed in a way that's angular or curvilinear, massive or delicate, traditional or avant-garde.

Which alternative is best? It's up to the designer to judge; the first principle in form development is that the form must satisfactorily express the piece's concept. A table intended to blend with a suite of traditional hardwood furniture would probably not work with an outlandish base, nor would a chair de-

FACING PAGE: The form of Pan Chair, designed by Vico Magistretti of Milan, Italy, suggests a seated person and was intended to relieve the emptiness of an unoccupied dining room. (Photo by Seth Stem.)

THIS PAGE: Above, the upholstered chair by Lee Trench of Roslindale, Mass., is inviting and conveys comfort and friendliness. In contrast, the angular chairs below by Charles Crowley of Waltham, Mass., have a high-tech, futuristic feel. (Photos by Dean Powell.)

signed to appear soft and comfortable warrant a strongly rectilinear or geometric form.

Subtle variations of a form can dramatically affect its visual message. Imagine a sphere attached to a wall. If the sphere is designed with a consistent curvature, it will look static, perhaps machined. If it is distorted to a slight pear shape, with most of its volume below the equator, it will look organic, as though it is responding to gravity (see the desk on p. 60). By contrast, if most of the sphere's volume is above the equator, the form will appear lightweight, on the brink of ascension. While all of these forms are fine, the choice of one over another should reflect goals specific to the concept.

The second principle of form development is that a form should have balance, either within itself or with another element. This does not mean that a form must be symmetrical, just that any variations should be counterbalanced. Forms shouldn't appear top-heavy or bottom-heavy without good reason. A designer must be able to feel when a form is balanced, rather than just engineer a physically balanced form, because the latter may be boring. So it is wise to be concerned with visual interest when exploring balance. The question of balance when designing a form ties in closely with the goals of composition (see pp. 82-99). A balanced form often automatically yields a balanced composition, but refer to pp. 87-89 to make sure the piece is interesting as well as balanced.

Third, emphasis on one or more parts is also important when considering form, because when there is variation within a form there will be dynamism— forms that are too consistent are likely to appear bland. Emphasis in form design is analogous to emphasis in a spoken sentence. Every sentence has a beginning, the development of a thought and ultimately an end, but at any point emphasis may be given through the choice of words or the ways the words are spoken. Similarly, emphasis can be added to any part of a form. The top drawing at right shows one treatment. The top table is rather uninteresting, because the legs have unvarying curvature and consistent thickness. Emphasizing the legs adds dynamism to the entire form. The legs of the bottom table have a well-defined beginning and end, a tighter radius toward the foot of the curve, and a variation in width.

For another example, consider the three lamps in the bottom drawing at right. The base and glass reflector of the first lamp are similarly sized; without emphasis of color or texture, they are about equal in importance. Enlarging the reflector and reducing the base, as in the second lamp, creates emphasis through a difference in scale. The third lamp uses the scale of

FACING PAGE, TOP: The forms of the base and top of this table by Amy Carson of Providence, R.I., are not particularly well balanced. The organic base flares upward and in itself is quite a lively structure, but it is poorly integrated with the form of the slate top. The thin plane of the top visually truncates the base and fails to balance its weight. Matters could have been improved by a better transition between the two components, by more overhang of the top and, of course, by a thicker top. (Photo by Seth Stem.)

FACING PAGE, BOTTOM: The overall form of this American-style Bombay chest (c. 1755-1795) feels uncomfortably bottom-heavy because of the bulging carcase sides and drawer fronts, which are opposed only by a thin top. (Photo courtesy Museum of Art, Rhode Island School of Design, bequest of Charles L. Pendleton.)

ADDING EMPHASIS TO ENLIVEN A TABLE FORM

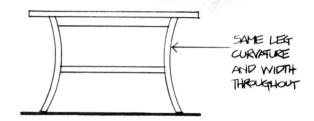

SAME LEG CURVATURE AND WIDTH THROUGHOUT

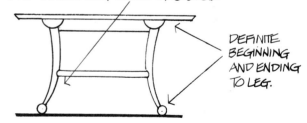

CURVE DEVELOPS TIGHTER RADIUS TOWARD FOOT, AND VARIOUS LEG WIDTHS ARE USED.

DEFINITE BEGINNING AND ENDING TO LEG.

ADDING EMPHASIS TO A LAMP

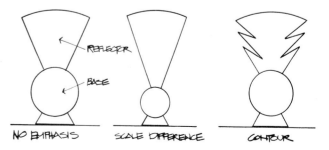

REFLECTOR

BASE

NO EMPHASIS   SCALE DIFFERENCE   CONTOUR

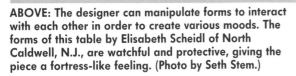

the first lamp, but adds emphasis through the active shape of the reflector. As you can see, emphasis in form is closely tied to emphasis in composition. However, form emphasis deals with contour and scale relationships, while composition concentrates primarily on placement.

A fourth principle of overall form design is that for maximum visual interest, a form should create relationships either within itself or with surrounding elements. In other words, forms should interact. Using forms sensitively creates a harmonious design, as shown in the photo above of the upholstered bench, while juxtaposing dissimilar forms in a disorderly or haphazard manner may give a chaotic feel.

Depending on their location and proximity to each other, forms can also be used to create a particular mood by suggesting tension, aggression and serenity, among other qualities. For example, the point of a triangular form directed at an adjacent rectangle feels aggressive; if a side of the same triangle is adjacent to the rectangle, the feeling changes because of the compatibility of the two adjacent

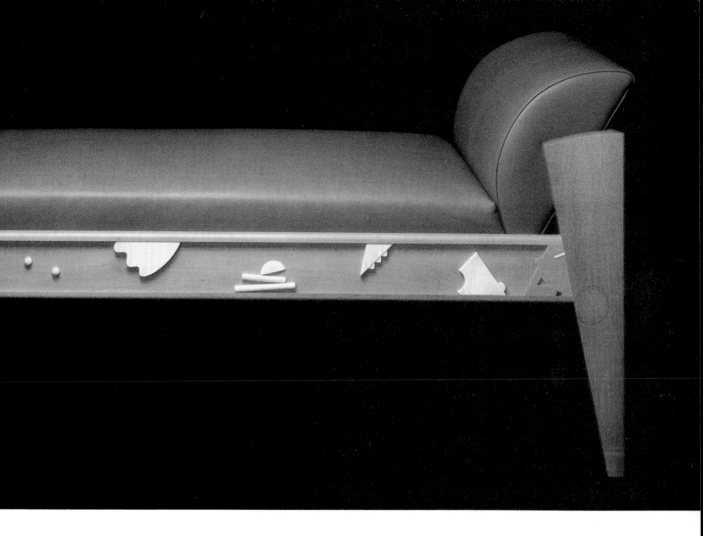

straight edges. Here again, the issues of form overlap those of composition.

Fifth, the form of a piece of furniture must be sensitive to the materials used. Always seek the most appropriate material for the form under design. If you want to use veneer, don't design a form with fragile edges or the piece will be at constant risk of damage. Consider, too, that the eye perceives certain relative weights for common materials, so a form attractive in wood might look unattractively massive if made the same size in steel.

Last, when designing the overall form of a piece, try to consider all viewing angles. Much too often, designers study only one view, usually the front view of a cabinet and the side view of a chair. In Cory Burr's chair on the facing page, it's clear that the side view (top photo) was the main focus; the front view (bottom photo) is less effective.

By contrast, the overall form of Arata Isozaki's chair (facing page, right) is much more successful. The side of the chair has a more active form than the front, but front-view interest is generated by the

BELOW: This jewelry box by Kingsley Brooks of Medford, Mass., is a nice form in itself, but not appropriate for veneering because the edges and corners are vulnerable to damage. (Photo by Larry Hunter.)

FACING PAGE, LEFT: Although there are relationships between the curvilinear forms throughout, this chair by Cory Burr of Providence, R.I., looks as though it were designed primarily from the side view. The curves introduced into the front view through the edges of the seat and back just don't have the same command and character as those in side view. (Photo by Seth Stem.)

FACING PAGE, RIGHT: The side view of the 'Marilyn Chair' by Arata Isozaki of Tokyo, Japan, is more active than the front, but the backrest slats in the front view also provide interest. (Photo courtesy MIT Hayden Gallery.)

long slats. Where it's not possible to strengthen an uninteresting form, the designer can use other elements of the visual vocabulary (such as texture or color) to compensate.

principles of detail form Because function and structure have already been considered in the overall form, there is more freedom in developing the details. Designs are most often successful if the detail shapes are consistent throughout a piece, for example, on the legs, armrests, back support and seat of a chair. (Of course the scale of the detailing has to change, depending on its location in the piece.) But not all details must relate closely. Contrast and variety are needed to keep a piece visually alive. Rounded-over edges on a curvilinear framework create a sculptural feel, whereas crisp edges add definition by creating shadow lines that visually separate planes and edges. The drawing below illustrates how

VARIOUS DETAIL FORMS IN A CHEST

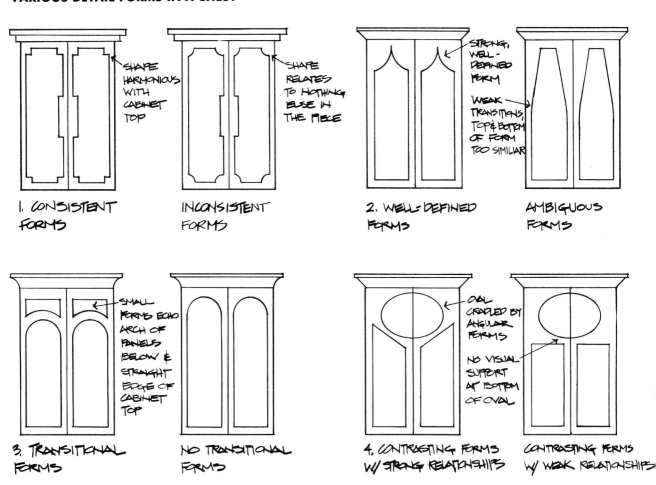

various details might work in a simple rectangular chest. In the first example, a strong relationship between forms is established in the consistent detailing of the doors and cabinet top. Rounding the door-panel corners weakens this relationship.

In the second example, the form of the panels on the left is well defined, but the panels on the right are weak. Here too much balance is a bad thing. The top of the form is too similar to the bottom, and the transition from the straight sides to the tapers is muddy and uninteresting.

The third example demonstrates how a piece can benefit from a transitional element. The smaller forms above the arches in the cabinet on the left pick up both the shape of the door panels and the horizontal line of the cabinet top, softening the contrast between the two.

The last example illustrates the importance of relationships between contrasting forms. In the cabinet on the left, the trapezoids seem to cradle the oval. This is much stronger than the relationship shown in the cabinet on the right, where the panels fail to interact with the oval. Here the oval is also surrounded by too much negative space; especially on the underside, it could use some visual support.

The key is to use detail form systematically. For example, the framework of a chair may be based on certain shapes, but if you think of the backrest as a complementary element framed by the chair structure, you can detail it entirely differently. The well-developed curvilinear profiles of the filing dividers in the writing desk at top right contrast nicely with the straightforward lines of the rest of the piece.

During design, consider adding transitions between detail forms so the jump from one form to another doesn't appear awkward or abrupt, especially when there is a change in materials. Introducing a small third detail between two existing forms is a good way to create a transition, as in the table at bottom right, where adding a small ring where the top of the cylindrical table leg ends in a ball effects a

TOP RIGHT: The curved forms of the file dividers of this desk by Louis Goodman of New York, N.Y., contrast sharply with the straightforward construction of the frame and become a focal point. (Photo courtesy Gallery of Applied Arts, New York, N.Y.)

RIGHT: The blue ring acts as a transitional form between the orange ball and the black leg top in this table, which was designed by Jack Larimore of Philadelphia, Pa. (Photo by Rick Echelmeyer.)

smooth transition. The form of a transitional element need not closely relate to the forms on either side, but scale is important. The transitional element is usually a lot smaller than the forms it separates; if it becomes too large, it becomes less of a transition and more of a form in its own right.

When designing detail forms, more is not necessarily better; there really is only so much information a viewer can digest before a piece becomes visually confusing. A good rule in evaluating whether a piece is fully developed is to try to subtract or add information—if doing either makes the piece less attractive, confuses the visual message or clouds the concept, it's a good bet the design is complete.

some form analyses Now let's look at some pieces in terms of the success or failure of their overall and detail forms. What follows is strictly my opinion, for creating a pleasing, dynamic form is much more than a matter of memorizing and adhering to a few guidelines. There is really no substitute for trial and error, or for heart and soul. Yet there will always be the form that is loved by one designer and loathed by another—both for good reason. If one of your pieces is ever at the heart of such a controversy, listen hard to all sides, because there is often as much to be learned from opinion as from fact.

First, consider the chair in the photo below. Its form is well balanced and uses several interior rela-

FACING PAGE: This Art Nouveau cabinet, designed c. 1899 by Hector Guimard, uses fluid, organic transitional forms where the curved linear elements meet the carcase sides. (Photo courtesy Virginia Museum of Fine Arts, collection of Sydney and Frances Lewis.)

BELOW: The form of Prom Chair by Jeff Kellar of Portland, Maine, gives a feeling of protection and security to the occupant. The overall quietness of the piece is given life through the voluptuous form of the seat. (Photo by Stretch Tuemmler.)

tionships to create and sustain visual interest. The upholstered shapes relate well to each other; the swelling of the seat, which is a dominant feature, reflects the more subtle padding of the sides and back. Thus there is similarity enough for harmony and variety enough for dynamism.

The transitions between the upholstered elements are also interesting. Note how the curves at the edges of the seat and sides come together tangentially, creating a downward, outward motion that helps break up the straight lines of the legs in front view. This is a clever use of form, in that the straight sides take on the interest of a more articulated shape. In addition, form here conveys information about how the user will feel when seated. The plush walls suggest protection and containment; the puffy seat implies comfort.

In contrast, the carcase of the desk in the photo at left is not nearly as successful. Although innovative in structure, it looks off balance and top-heavy, with the egg-shaped sides appearing to succumb to gravitational forces. In addition, the forms of the sides (and front, when closed) lack depth, and read as elevations rather than three-dimensional objects. They are just too plain for the scale of the piece.

Probably the desk could be improved by a heavier base, which would balance the heaviness of the carcase. A heavier base would also counteract the impression of structural tenuousness created by cantilevering the carcase over the base (although the base is certainly sturdily constructed). The understructure would also benefit from a transitional element to receive the egg shapes. The interior of the desk is quite appealing in form and detail, but some variation in compartment spacing would help break up the repetition.

The small round-top table in the photo on the facing page has an extremely successful linear form. It is well balanced and dynamic, and there are lots of things to keep the eye engrossed. The interesting leg curves end with a well-defined base that changes di-

LEFT: The overall form of Egg Desk by David Powell of East Hampton, Mass., is top-heavy and lacks depth. In contrast, the subtle curvature of the interior and the composition of drawers and cubbyholes are quite pleasing. (Photo by Robert Aude.)

FACING PAGE: Bruce Volz of East Hampton, Mass., produced an extremely pleasing active form with the linear base of this table. Interesting interior relationships hold the viewer's eye. (Photo by David Ryan.)

rection to create a foot. The tight curves of the foot and base segue into the gentle curve of the legs and appear to be releasing a great deal of tension, visually pushing the table upward. The tops of the legs come to a definite end just above the table surface, and the table inlay picks up the leg color for a pleasing interior relationship.

The overall form of the secretary on the facing page was sensitively designed in the way it steps in along its profiles—obviously in the front with the slanted writing-surface lid, and subtly along the sides with the protruding feet and the way the two main cabinet sections are offset. All this helps prevent the creation of an overbearing, imposing presence.

However, this piece could have profited from a little more definition. Given the collective weight of the base, drawers and cabinet, the cornice appears insignificantly small, creating a feeling of bottom-heaviness. The feet, by contrast, have a pleasing relationship with the cabinet base, because they extend outward from the carcase, suggesting stability. Also, the curves of the feet blend nicely with the bottom moldings. Widening the top molding would have strengthened the cornice form and developed more mass with which to balance the door panels and base.

Too much form information can detract from the main focus of a piece, as in the five-drawer chest at right. The concept of the piece was to construct a chest with curved drawer sides and tracking that allowed the drawer to pull out in an arc. The structural basis of the chest is three coved support columns that connect horizontal planes between the drawers, so the forms of the drawers themselves are exposed. The columns and drawers have an architectural look, but adding the freeform bentwood elements and sculptural-looking base leads to visual confusion. The conceptual point (curved drawers) is subverted, and no form element is dominant because the bentwood sweep, the base and the basic structure all compete for attention.

FACING PAGE: Unity in the design of this 18th-century secretary by Job Townsend of Newport, R.I., comes from the consistent stepping in along the profiles of the writing-surface lid and the feet. Yet the cornice appears too light to counterbalance the weight of the base. This is an example of detail form causing bottom-heaviness in a piece. (Photo courtesy Museum of Art, Rhode Island School of Design, gift of Mrs. Murray S. Danforth.)

RIGHT: In this chest by Seth Stem, too much form information overrides the concept of curved drawers, which the piece was to illustrate. (Photo by Seth Stem.)

elements that influence form

The design of a form clearly can be affected by elements a designer selects from the visual vocabulary. The influence can be blatant, as when a designer experiments with the posture of a piece, or subtle, as when composition or color visually alters the proportions of a form. For the rest of this chapter we will explore the more obvious influences on form, noting in subsequent chapters how other elements of the visual vocabulary work to alter form.

line weight   Almost all types of furniture contain linear elements, whether they form the structure of a chair frame, the edge of a tabletop or the rails and stiles of a carcase. These linear elements have a visual width, which I call line weight. When you work out the form of a piece, you'd obviously also rough out the linear elements, but you really should pay them close attention. This is because line weight does much to influence the appearance of a piece.

   In furniture, as in drawings, line weight is useful for establishing a visual hierarchy—thick, dominant lines contrasted with thinner, secondary lines tell the viewer what is important and what is less so. In the first chest in the drawing below, the lines of the carcase frame are thicker and heavier than the partition lines between drawers. The dominant form of

LINE WEIGHT IN TWO CHESTS

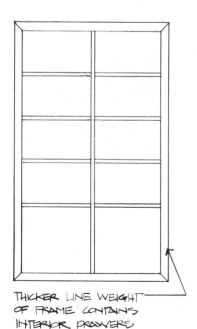

THICKER LINE WEIGHT
OF FRAME CONTAINS
INTERIOR DRAWERS

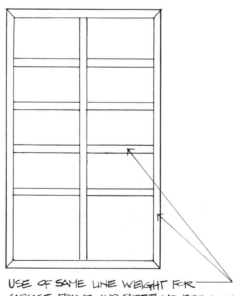

USE OF SAME LINE WEIGHT FOR
CARCASE FRAME AND PARTITIONS BETWEEN
DRAWERS RESULTS IN AN UNREFINED APPEARANCE

the structure therefore contains the interior components. In the second chest, however, there is no such containment of interior elements; the result is awkwardness and a lack of refinement.

However, consistent line weights need not be a liability if they are used in a design where there are dominant and subordinate forms. For example, consider the two pieces shown here. The chair, which has a clean, highly controlled look, uses essentially the same line weight throughout its frame and back slats. This chair is dominated by the tall form of the back, the upward thrust of which is nicely capped by the dense top grid. Although the stool was nicely made with hand-cut joints, its use of similar line weights throughout is much less successful since there is no dominant form. No distinction has been made between the seat and the base, or between the frame of the seat and the slats, or even among the structural members of the base. Either the creation of a dominant form or an alteration in the line weight of some of the members would have made the overall form of this piece more visually interesting.

RIGHT: Charles Rennie Mackintosh's Hill House chair uses about the same line weight throughout, but the increased density of lines through a grid at the top creates a definite cap to the chair's upward motion. (Photo courtesy Cassina S.p.A.)

BELOW: The line weight in this stool by Bill Sloane of Rochester, N.Y., is so consistent it lacks interest. Either a dominant form or a variety of leg sizes would have created a more dynamic piece. (Photo by Andrew Olenick.)

CHANGING PERCEIVED THICKNESS THROUGH VARIOUS EDGE TREATMENTS

SQUARE EDGE HAS UTILITARIAN CHARACTER.

COVE REDUCES AREA, PROVIDES SHADOW UNDERNEATH TO VISUALLY REDUCE EDGE.

BEADING PROVIDES SMALLER SURFACES AND A VARIETY OF FORMS, GIVING A REFINED APPEARANCE.

CHAMFER INCREASES EDGE SURFACE, GIVES BOLDER, WEIGHTIER LOOK.

SEVERE UNDERCUT GIVES DELICATE LOOK TO TOP, DISGUISES THICKNESS.

Heavy line weights support massive forms, lighter line weights give a feeling of delicacy. Make sure that the line weights you use in a piece complement its overall character. In the jewelry chest shown below, for example, the line weight of the base is just too heavy for the scale of the tamboured chest. The chest is composed of many delicate lines—the thin tambour slats, interior partitions and carcase edges—all of which contrast with the wide, flat, utilitarian-looking legs. The result is a lack of cohesion in the design.

The drawing at left shows how a tabletop's edge detailing can dramatically change its perceived line weight. It is also possible to disguise actual thickness by radically undercutting an edge, as long as the edge can be viewed from above a point of true ele-

BELOW: The line weight of the legs of this jewelry chest is much too heavy for the delicacy of the carcase. (Photo by Seth Stem.)

FACING PAGE: The stepped edge of this chair, designed by Abel Faidy, is not only an interesting form in its own right, but it also interacts aggressively with the negative space around it. (Photo by Abramson-Culbert Studio, courtesy Chicago Historical Society.)

vation. This illustrates the importance of the viewing angle and how it can affect the perceived weight of furniture parts. Very often, everything looks harmonious and in proportion when a piece is drawn from a front or side view. But once the piece is made, it will rarely be viewed as it was drawn, strictly in elevation. When seen from an angle, certain elements may appear heavier or awkward. (This happens because the diagonal dimension can be larger than the face dimension.)

positive and negative space Furniture is usually designed by consciously manipulating positive forms. It's easy to forget that any positive area has a negative space with which it interacts. This negative space can be as important to the form as the positive area, because it can act as a backdrop for the image, form a distinct image of its own, or be read as a volume if positive forms surround it. Because the shape of the positive form is reflected by the shape of the negative space, they have the effect of reinforcing each other. When manipulating the positive form, evaluate how the negative space is strengthened or weakened. Look at the chair at right. The negative space enclosed by the legs and armrests enhances the base's boxiness. In addition, the stepped edges of the back aggressively agitate the negative space around it. If the back were smooth and rounded, this chair would have an entirely different feeling.

Just as you can use the relationship of positive to negative space to alter the feeling of a piece, you can also create different effects by varying the proportion of positive to negative spaces. In the end view of the table in the drawing below, the first frame surrounds a large, rectangular negative space,

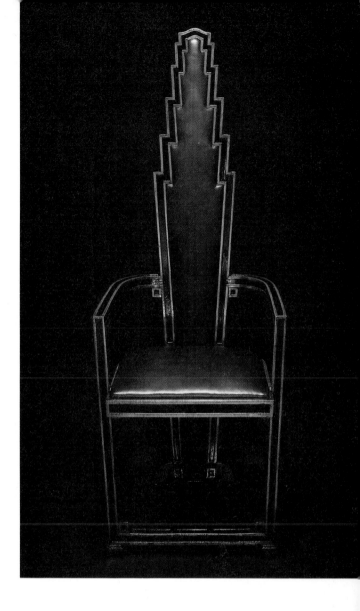

PROPORTIONING NEGATIVE SPACE

LARGE AREA OF NEGATIVE SPACE FEELS INCONSEQUENTIAL.

SMALLER AREA SUGGESTS SOMETHING IMPORTANT IS CONTAINED.

SMALLEST AREA REDUCES IN IMPORTANCE TO THE STATUS OF A HOLE.

THE EFFECT OF DENSITY ON PERCEIVED LINE WEIGHT

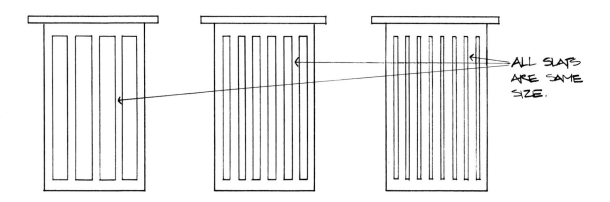

ALL SLATS ARE SAME SIZE.

VARYING FORM OF NEGATIVE SPACE

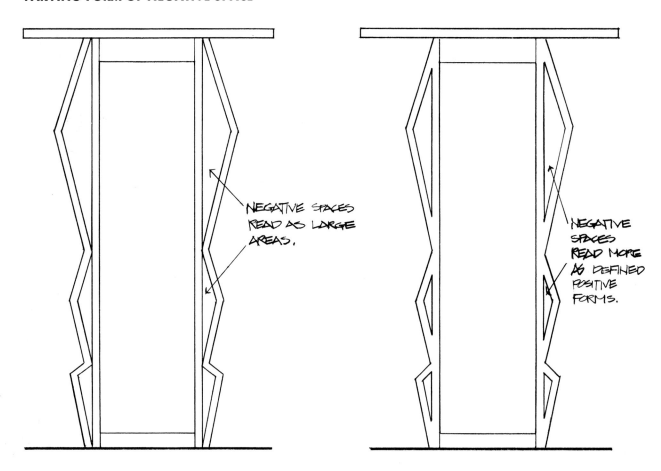

NEGATIVE SPACES READ AS LARGE AREAS.

NEGATIVE SPACES READ MORE AS DEFINED POSITIVE FORMS.

which feels vast and inconsequential. As the frame is made more substantial, the negative space also grows in importance—the heaviness of the form implies that the interior space contains something important or leads to something intriguing. But if the size of the frame increases even more, as in the third table, the effect begins to reverse and the negative space is so overwhelmed that it becomes unimportant. Generally it's true that if a strong separation occurs between an inside and outside negative space, the inside negative space gains importance and the outside negative space acts as background. Density can also be controlled by the relationship of positive and negative space, as shown in the top drawing on the facing page. As negative space decreases, the visual weight changes from light to heavy.

How comfortable we are in perceiving individual negative spaces sometimes depends on their form and proximity. Consider the bottom drawing on the facing page. Both of the tables have similar angular bases, but in the one on the right there is a definite separation of negative spaces, while in the one on the left, the issue is somewhat undefined. The negative spaces of the left base therefore read as one large, extended area, whereas the spaces in the base on the right read as repetitious triangular forms. Each example can be used effectively to promote the intent of the designer.

directionality Designers create directionality in a piece for many reasons, most often to impart visual motion or to call attention to a special detail or function. Establishing a strong sense of direction is a good way to guide viewers through the use of a piece, just as good architecture gives visual clues as to where the main entrance and elevators are.

Obviously, directionality can be created through a piece's form (and the elements within it), as in the table at right, as well as through composition. But it can also be generated through use of the other design elements, such as ornamentation and color. Color, for instance, could graduate from light to dark across the length of a tabletop, or graduate to focus on a central point. Both methods would draw the eye across the piece. (For more on color, see pp. 106-117.)

The large triangular form of this occasional table by Wendy Maruyama, of Oakland, Calif., has a strong downward thrust. The three tilted rubber drawer pulls seem to be falling into the vessel-like form. (Photo by Seth Stem.)

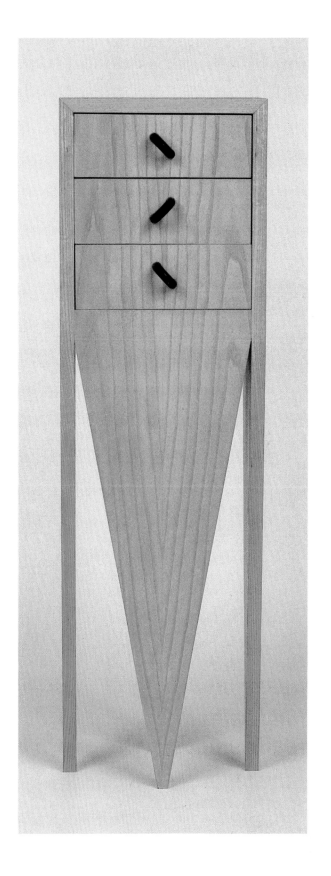

Each chair in the photo below has a strong directionality. The center and right chairs imply motion through the slats, flooding the senses with verticals and horizontals. Here the directional elements—the slats—are integrated with and sympathetic to the chair form; they emphasize the vertical or horizontal axis of the structure. The visual strength of the chair at left is gained by contrasting the directional element with the overall form. The number of slats also affects directional impact. If the chair on the right had only three horizontal slats for a backrest and one stretcher under the seat, visual activity would be dramatically reduced. In the center chair, subtle form variation accentuates directionality. If the backrest were not flared at the top, vertical direction would still be evident, but not nearly as strongly.

Sometimes the form of the functional parts of a piece of furniture can imply movement and direction. Look at the teacarts on the facing page. In the cart at top, the curved handles and back legs form an "arrowhead" pointing toward the front of the cart, telling the user which way and where to push. This cart looks active even when at rest. By contrast, the cart at bottom looks static because the forms read primarily as straight verticals and horizontals.

animation and posture   When a piece takes on
the appearance of something alive or possesses a
quality relating to a human or animal form or action,
I call it animated. This quality can be realized in furniture through the use of forms that allude to human
or animal members, especially feet and legs. As the
photos here show, these forms can subtly hint at anthropomorphic qualities or can be highly abstracted
or stylized, but they are usually not a direct repre-
sentation of a live subject, for then the piece would
be the image of an animal itself.

The table at the bottom of the facing page uses
directionality to promote an animated quality, but it
also has characteristics of a bird-dog stance. Had the
piece been designed so that the legs on the right
side were not offset from the legs on the left (the
tabletop is a parallelogram, not a rectangle), the
piece would probably be only directional. As it is,
the legs point, like a setter at a quail, and bring the
table to life. As you can see, forms do not necessarily
have to be organic to introduce animation. This table
is actually quite the opposite.

In the same way that each person has a posture,
so the form of a furniture piece may appear proud,
sagging, upright or energetic. At right are two pieces
of furniture with contrasting postures. The 18th-
century Chippendale card table suggests the dignity
and strength of a soldier on guard, but the chair looks
like it is slouching on its front legs. Sometimes the
subtle shaping or angling of an element can change
the entire posture of a piece. For example, if the legs
of a table were tilted slightly inward, the posture
might indicate instability; if the legs were tilted out,
the posture would convey strength and solidity.

FACING PAGE, TOP: The liveliness of the leg forms of
this desk by Jere Osgood, of Wilton, N.H., gives the
piece an animated quality. (Photo by Michael Germer.)

FACING PAGE, BOTTOM: The angular form of this table
by Ken Byrne of Providence, R.I., both creates directionality
and suggests a bird dog stalking its quarry. The surface is
made of a maple grid in which are set bent tabs of painted
steel, all oriented the same way. (Photo by Seth Stem.)

ABOVE RIGHT: This 18th-century Chippendale card
table has the attentive posture of a soldier on guard.
(Photo courtesy Museum of Art, Rhode Island School of
Design, bequest of Charles L. Pendleton.)

RIGHT: The posture of this chair suggests a steer being
dragged to slaughter. (Photo courtesy State University of
Buffalo, N.Y.)

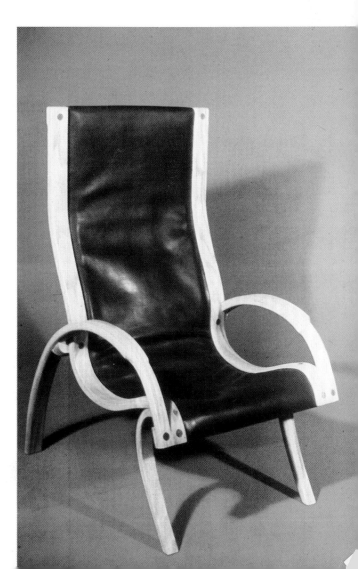

LINE AND CIRCLE INTERACTION

WHEN THE LINE IS CENTERED ON THE CIRCLE, THE INTERACTION SEEMS SATISFYING - SOLID AND COMFORTABLE.

BY CONTRAST, THIS RELATIONSHIP SEEMS AWKWARD AND INDECISIVE.

WHEN THE LINE IS AT A TANGENT TO THE CIRCLE, THE RELATIONSHIP IS ALSO VISUALLY COMFORTABLE.

THE SPIRAL CONFIGURATION IS SMOOTH AND FLOWING

THIS RELATIONSHIP SEEMS INTERRUPTED, NOT FLOWING SMOOTHLY.

THE WAVY LINE EVENTUALLY MEETING THE CIRCLE GIVES A FEELING OF PLEASANT ANTICIPATION.

WHEN THE LINE APPEARS TO PENETRATE THE CIRCLE, THE EFFECT IS SYMMETRICAL, LOGICAL, VISUALLY COMFORTABLE.

MORE THAN ONE LINE INTERSECTING THE CIRCLE INDICATES THE CIRCLE IS A CONNECTING POINT. DIRECTING THE LINES TO THE CENTER OF THE CIRCLE MAKES THEM FEEL CONTINUOUS AND VISUALLY STRONG.

To eliminate unpleasant surprises, try to anticipate posture problems by using drawings, models or mockups while designing. I've seen otherwise elegant work spoiled by bulldog legs, and pieces that have an unattractive air of terminal fatigue. Work toward having your pieces project self-respect and pride.

line/form interaction The way the eye is accustomed to perceiving objects in nature and in everyday life creates a visual logic to which we unconsciously respond. Designs that conform to this logic seem comfortable; designs that violate it appear awkward. Consider the diagrams at left of a line and a circle, and the degree of visual satisfaction in the ways they interact.

Some styles of furniture require that a linear framework interact with other forms, such as carcases, bases and upholstered areas. The intersection of the frame (viewed as a line), and another form will be more successful if it is based on some sort of logic. Random intersections cry out for justification. Aligning or centering elements, creating square intersections or using any other logical relationship will usually help organize furniture parts and enhance the appeal of the design, even if the relationship is not apparent to the viewer. Beware of over-organization, however; it is not the goal to have a viewer notice a piece's orderliness and none of its

FACING PAGE, LEFT: T-Bird 56 by Dakota Jackson of New York, N.Y., has interesting relationships between lines and forms. The way the linear supports intersect the cylinders underneath the desktop is logical, but how they meet the base is not. (Photo by Maseo Ueda.)

FACING PAGE, TOP: The inlaid lines in the back of this chair by Peter Dean of Charlestown, Mass., align with the inside edges of the back legs, creating a logical relationship with the chair form. The inlaid square at the bottom of the line also is logically placed, centered on the width of the side stretcher. (Photo by Morse Peterson.)

FACING PAGE, BOTTOM: Hugh Scriven of Northants, England, designed his Joe Wright Cabinet with line/form interaction and centering in mind. The veneered triangles on the doors are evenly divided by the line formed by the intersection of each set of doors, and this line also is centered on the triangular base forms. In this case, lining up elements may have been carried out too literally in the triangular bases, because their position, while logical, results in too much carcase overhang on both sides, creating a feeling of precariousness. Centering the base forms on the outside door panels would have relieved this problem. (Photo by Hugh Scriven.)

intrigue. To be pleasant to view, a design need not be obvious.

In the desk shown below, the ingenious outrigger tabletop supports consist of metal rods that intersect cylindrical forms under the tabletop. The arrangement is logical, in that the rods connect to the center of the cylindrical forms. No complementary logic, however, governs the way the supports intersect with the sharply sloping sides of the base. The physically difficult connection between these round support rods and the flat-surfaced base contributes to the feeling of visual discomfort.

scale Scale is the perceived relationship of the size of an object or design element to its surroundings, another object or adjacent elements. Scale is very closely related to proportion (pp. 92-105), but I like to distinguish between the two. To me scale relates to relative mass, in how we view an object in relationship to our own scale as human beings and in how we view parts of an object within its entirety. I talk about the scale of a drawer pull in relationship to the drawer or the entire chest in terms of whether it looks big or small. I talk about the proportions of the same drawer pull in terms of width versus length. To me, proportion is a mathematical notion—a measurement of one part or side of an object in relation to another part or side—while scale is a visual evaluation and reaction based on mass.

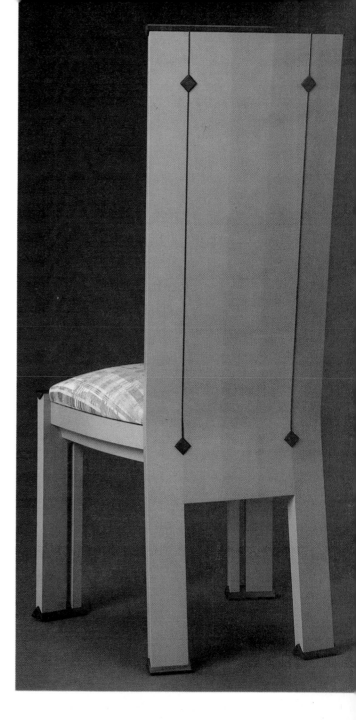

How scale is manipulated can drastically affect the appearance of a piece. Consider the two chests of drawers shown here. Both are about the same overall size. But while the highboy on the facing page appears monolithic, the traditional-style dresser at right has a much lighter feel. This is because the form and scale of each part of the highboy were exaggerated yet all components were kept simple—the legs are large, unadorned columns continuing from floor to cornice, the separation between drawers is minimal, and the heavy cornice is made from a single shape of molding, increasing the look of mass. In contrast, the distinctly defined drawers on the traditional dresser break up the central area, and the carcase outline has a much lighter line weight. Hardware and detailing, such as the legs, also interrupt the viewer's eye, reducing visual mass.

Form, detailing and line weight can influence how the overall scale of a piece is perceived. For example, the scale of the piece at the top of the facing page is deceiving because the rounded-over forms are coupled with consistent line weight. The two intersecting lines of the structure are so simple that they don't give the viewer many visual clues about size. Though the piece looks as if it could be held in the palm of the hand, it is actually a stool, with the bump on the arch forming the seat and the bar at the bottom the footrest.

You can alter the perceived scale of any component by interrupting its surface through carving, fluting, grooving or decorating. Giving the eye more to comprehend within a limited area generally reduces the scale of that area. On the secretary on p. 78, the carvings of the door panels and fold-down writing surface break up the surfaces and visually diminish the size of the piece.

FACING PAGE, TOP: The scale of this piece is deceiving. It appears that it could be held in the palm of the hand, but the large, rounded forms of laminated mahogany, created by Joseph Distefano, actually shape a stool. (Photo courtesy Virginia Commonwealth University.)

FACING PAGE, BOTTOM: Simple exaggerated forms in this highboy by Joe Duke, of New York, N.Y., emphasize its mass. (Photo courtesy Gallery of Applied Art, New York, N.Y.)

RIGHT: Even though the size of this traditional-style dresser is about the same as the one on the facing page, the defined drawers, lighter line weight and use of detailing reduce visual mass. (Photo by Seth Stem, courtesy Cabot House.)

light and shadow All forms are affected by light and shadow. Changes in planes read as a sharp line because of the differences in light intensity from a dominant light source; rounded forms read as such because the changes in light intensity appear as a gradation from light to dark. Light and shadow can visually activate a piece of furniture by highlighting and defining components and edges. Shapes, reveals, recesses and texture become evident when appropriate shadows are created, and can be used to break up or separate areas of a form. Sometimes light reflected off a rounded or spherical form can give life to that element. Any element that is crisp and defined can benefit from a strong shadowline.

When you are considering light and shadow, take into account any patterns, color, edges and overhangs. Light colors tend to make shadows more apparent. Defined forms and crisp edges give a clean break between highlighted and shadowed areas, especially where there is directional lighting. Patterns usually do better if they receive uniform light, so the image reads without interruption—avoid overhangs in this situation. Relief carvings usually need shadows in order to read well, so light-colored woods may be a more appropriate choice. The outline of drawers and doors can sometimes be strengthened by the shadowline created by a slight recess. Darkening a recessed area with paint or stain will make it read better because less light is reflected from the darker surface. The deeper a recess, as in a recessed drawer pull, the darker the shadow, and the sharper the form will read. Dull or matte surfaces will absorb light and look soft. Shiny surfaces will reflect light and may cause glare on the surface, which can block out wood grain, color or patterns, so be aware of the effect.

ABOVE LEFT: The beautiful scallop-shell carvings in this 18th-century Goddard-Townsend secretary from Newport, R.I., break up the surface of the door panels, thereby reducing their apparent scale. (Photo courtesy Museum of Art, Rhode Island School of Design, bequest of Martha B. Lisle.)

FACING PAGE: The shadowline under the top of this desk by Brian Gulick of New York, N.Y., makes the top seem to float and clearly separates it from the base. Gulick constructed the overhang so it would produce this shadowline in almost any lighting situation. (Photo by Brian Gulick.)

composition and proportion

All forms require attention to composition and proportion. Composition refers to the arrangement of forms within an object or the arrangement of elements within a form; proportion is the relationship of parts to each other or to the whole. These most important elements of the visual vocabulary can strengthen and refine a piece of furniture. Ignoring them, even in the details, invites serious design error.

Designers usually address the composition and proportion of a piece in the earliest stages of development. While sketching various forms, quickly try out different arrangements of components, heights and widths to explore various options. Putting the design into a scale drawing as soon as possible and overlaying sketches of different compositional and proportional relationships make it easier to determine the most appropriate solutions—the key to good composition is often simply the evaluation of options. It's inevitable, however, that refinements and even changes in design will occur down the road, especially when the piece is first seen in three dimensions as a model or mockup (see pp. 186-191).

principles of composition

In furniture design, composition is mostly a matter of trying to achieve balance, although it can deliberately be used to create imbalance. Composition deals with balance on two axes—from side to side and from top to bottom. The balance from side to side of a vertical centerline is usually the most visu-

Strong compositional relationships exist in this cabinet designed by Julius Hyde of London, England, and built by Ron Lenthall. With the doors closed (left), the matched veneer panels form squares that relate to the framework of the base. Opening the outside doors reveals a strong diagonal pattern on the interior doors radiating from a central opening (facing page), giving great importance to whatever is displayed there. The bottom diagonals also relate to the lines of the base. (Photos by Julius Hyde.)

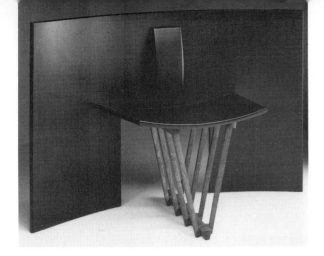

ally important, but a piece is not completely balanced unless it is balanced on both axes.

Balance can be divided into three categories: formal balance (symmetry), informal balance (asymmetry) and radial balance. These terms are widely used in the fields of art and design to help direct the evolution of a composition. The term formal balance probably came about historically from paintings, where the subject of greatest importance was placed in the center of the composition, with balancing subjects on either side. In formal balance, the design elements are either equally distributed or close to

ABOVE: The composition of this chair by Tom Hucker of Charlestown, Mass., has great symmetry and balance. The large bent-plywood curve acts as a backdrop to the smaller seat and backrest, which are of similar curvature and color. (Photo by Dean Powell.)

RIGHT: This upholstered aluminum couch by Charles Crowley of Waltham, Mass., is composed symmetrically. The formality of the materials, used here with great precision, creates strongly defined geometric shapes, some of which are framed by an outline of aluminum (as is the backrest) to reinforce the geometric form. (Photo by Dean Powell.)

FACING PAGE, TOP: The different-sized armrest bolsters of this asymmetrical loveseat by Kalle Fauset of New York, N.Y., provide balance. Using an odd number of bolsters on the right creates an informal, natural composition. (Photo by Seth Stem.)

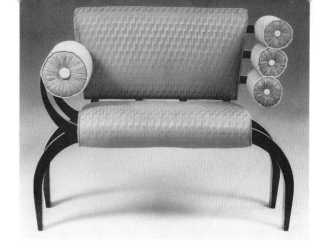

being equally distributed. A composition that is vertically divided in half, and in which one side is a reflection of the other, is symmetrical.

Asymmetry generally lends itself to less formal designs, because there is an interplay between elements and masses of different sizes and forms. For example, a large mass on one side of a piece might be counterbalanced by several smaller elements on the other, as in the loveseat at right. One of the exciting aspects of asymmetrical design is the potential to develop tensions between elements and to produce an extremely dynamic form.

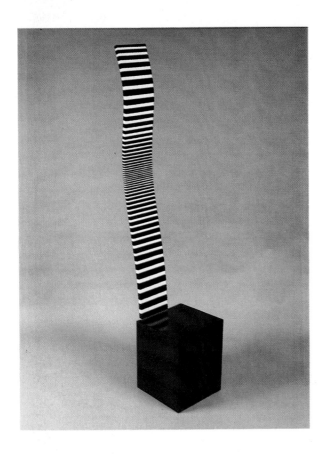

Radial balance occurs when elements radiate from a central source, like spokes on a wheel. The overall form, however, need not be circular—it can be oval, square, rectangular or triangular. Each of these forms has a central point from which a composition can radiate. As long as the radiating forms are the same or have the same rhythm, the composition created is naturally symmetrical no matter what form is selected. In furniture, radial symmetry can be used effectively not only in tabletops, but anywhere a central point can be established, such as in a mirror frame or an arched cabinet door.

When working on a composition, keep in mind that each design element will have its own visual value, which can enhance or undermine your efforts to balance the piece. Visual value is determined by the impact an element has on the eye. A large element has greater visual value than a small one; isolated elements typically have a greater impact than clustered ones, as shown in the drawing below left.

The color of an element (or its black or white value), also affects visual value. A vivid turquoise is more eye-catching than pastel blue, and plain black or white can have as strong a visual value as the most vibrant color. Materials influence visual value, too. In the top table on the facing page, for example, you can see that the visual value of the curly maple

LEFT: The stripes on the back of this chair by Julie Morengello of Providence, R.I., have a visual value as strong as the most vibrant color. (Photo by Seth Stem.)

FACING PAGE, TOP: In this table by Bryan Smallman of Norwalk, Conn., the curly maple balances the composition through its high visual value. (Photo by Bill West.)

FACING PAGE, BOTTOM: Radial symmetry is created in this conference table by Peter Dean of Charlestown, Mass., through the use of matched veneers, inlays and a circular base. (Photo by Dean Powell.)

ADDING VISUAL VALUE THROUGH ISOLATING ELEMENTS

ISOLATED INLAY ON RIGHT HAS GREATER VISUAL VALUE THAN CLUSTER ON LEFT.

DRAWER GROUPING ON LEFT IS BALANCED BY SIMILAR SIZED, BUT DIFFERENTLY SHAPED, DRAWER ON THE RIGHT. ITS ISOLATION MAKES IT PROMINENT IN COMPOSITION.

BALANCING A COMPOSITION

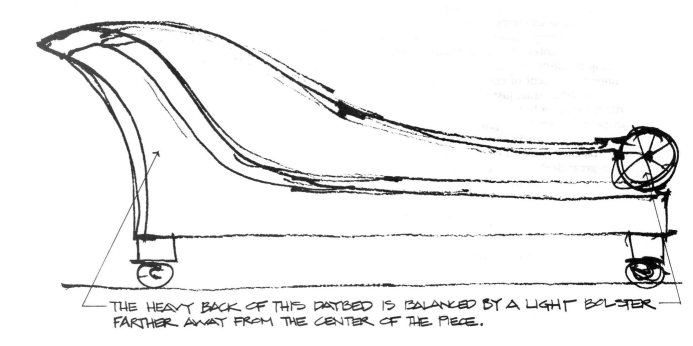

THE HEAVY BACK OF THIS DAYBED IS BALANCED BY A LIGHT BOLSTER FARTHER AWAY FROM THE CENTER OF THE PIECE.

THE EFFECT OF SCALE IN BALANCING A COMPOSITION

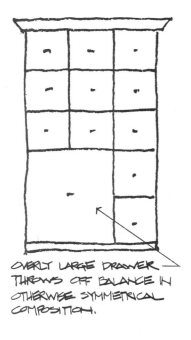

OVERLY LARGE DRAWER THROWS OFF BALANCE IN OTHERWISE SYMMETRICAL COMPOSITION.

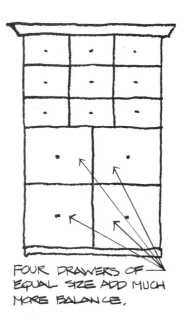

FOUR DRAWERS OF EQUAL SIZE ADD MUCH MORE BALANCE.

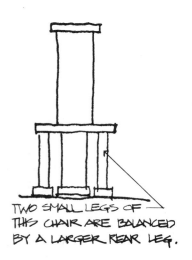

TWO SMALL LEGS OF THIS CHAIR ARE BALANCED BY A LARGER REAR LEG.

is greater than the visual value of the wenge used for the legs. A compositional balance is therefore created between the table feet and the top/apron.

The visual value of an element also depends on its placement in the composition. The farther the element is from the center, the more visual weight it has. Balancing an off-center element does not necessarily require an element of equal value in the same position on the other side, just a counterbalance. As with a balance scale, a heavy object close to the fulcrum can be balanced by a lighter object a greater distance away, as shown in the top drawing on the facing page. Balance can also be achieved by using a form with a great deal of activity or intense color.

Balance is also affected by the scale of various elements. As shown in the bottom drawing on the facing page, in a three-legged chair, the two smaller front legs might be balanced by a large leg in the rear. But in an otherwise symmetrical chest, an extreme variation in drawer size could create an imbalance in the composition.

The preceding information makes it fairly easy to analyze the composition of any furniture piece, but it doesn't provide any criteria for making a composition visually interesting. Also, if too much homage is paid to balance, the resulting design may be dull. I think it's important to establish a dialog between a piece and its viewer, and if a composition is too predictable, it won't hold the viewer's interest. It's therefore desirable to stimulate and involve the viewer with some sort of visual challenge. For example, consider the cabinets in the drawing at right. All are well balanced, but the first chest is bland, repetitious and too easy to understand. If the four doors have to remain the same size, composition can be improved by concentrating the handles in one area, as shown in the second chest, to produce a focal point that relieves the monotony of the equally sized doors. If the doors can be of different sizes, as in the third chest, the result is more stimulating.

The simple lamp in the photo on p. 88 is a fine example of good composition. Called Lamp Mercure, it is a collage of modernity and mythology, based on the god Mercury, who is traditionally depicted wearing winged sandals and carrying a winged staff with two entwined serpents. The placement of two-thirds of the circular diffusing disc below the top edge of the winged reflector creates a balanced but interesting symmetrical composition where all the elements appear to interact. What happens when you reposition the forms? In the top design in the drawing on p. 88, the reflector seems visually lost when the disc doesn't fill the space between the wings. What protrusion there is of the disc above the reflector looks weak. The alternative

COMPOSING A CABINET FOR VISUAL INTEREST

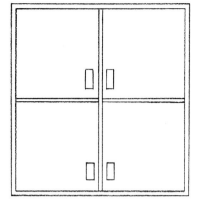

THIS CHEST IS OVERBALANCED, AND THEREFORE VISUALLY BLAND.

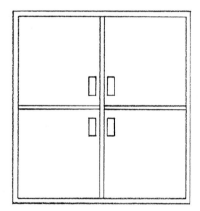

GROUPING THE HANDLES CLOSELY TOGETHER ADDS VISUAL INTEREST.

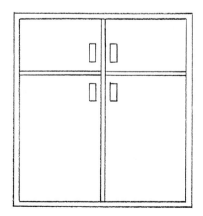

CHANGING THE DOOR SIZES GREATLY HEIGHTENS VISUAL INTEREST.

TWO ALTERNATIVE DESIGNS

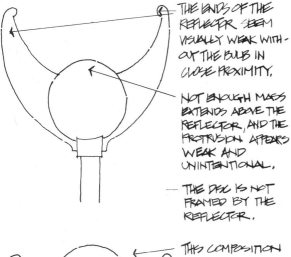

THE ENDS OF THE REFLECTOR SEEM VISUALLY WEAK WITHOUT THE BULB IN CLOSE PROXIMITY.

NOT ENOUGH MASS EXTENDS ABOVE THE REFLECTOR, AND THE PROTRUSION APPEARS WEAK AND UNINTENTIONAL.

— THE DISC IS NOT FRAMED BY THE REFLECTOR.

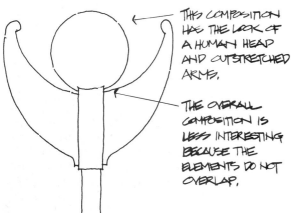

THIS COMPOSITION HAS THE LOOK OF A HUMAN HEAD AND OUTSTRETCHED ARMS.

THE OVERALL COMPOSITION IS LESS INTERESTING BECAUSE THE ELEMENTS DO NOT OVERLAP.

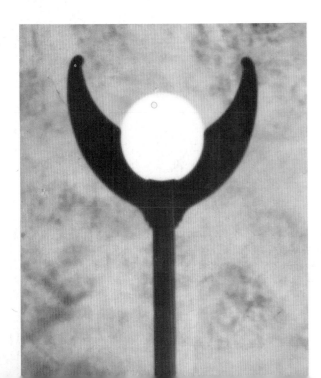

composition shown in the drawing bears a resemblance to Mighty Mouse, which makes a cartoonish statement rather than a mythological one. Also, because the reflector and the disc don't overlap, the forms don't interact, and the composition is much less interesting. These options are not nearly as successful as the original design.

Visual interest in a composition can sometimes be heightened by concentrating on its top, front or side view alone. For example, adding leg articulation to the bland plan view of the round table in the drawing below creates a more engrossing composition. When you add interest to one view in this way, the overall view of the piece is usually enhanced as well.

An interesting symmetrical composition results from the interaction of the circular diffusing disc and winged reflector in Lamp Mercure by Patrick Nagar of New York, N.Y. (Photo by Deidi von Schaewen, courtesy The Gallery of Applied Arts, New York, N.Y.)

ADDING COMPOSITIONAL INTEREST

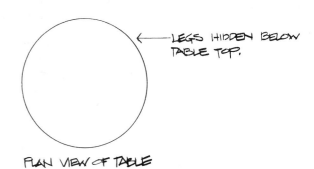

LEGS HIDDEN BELOW TABLE TOP.

PLAN VIEW OF TABLE

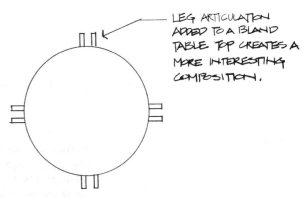

LEG ARTICULATION ADDED TO A BLAND TABLE TOP CREATES A MORE INTERESTING COMPOSITION.

PLAN VIEW OF TABLE

Visual interest is affected by the interplay of negative space and positive mass (see pp. 67-69). In a carcase piece mass is primary, but in a chair the spaces contained by the framework are compositional elements as well. Composition is also influenced by linear elements and their visual thickness, or line weight (pp. 64-67), and the way they are arranged. In the first table in the drawing below, the mirror-image stretchers create a symmetrical, classic mood. In the second table, the stretchers echo the bow of the apron, and create a pendulous posture.

THE EFFECT OF LINEAR ELEMENTS ON COMPOSITION

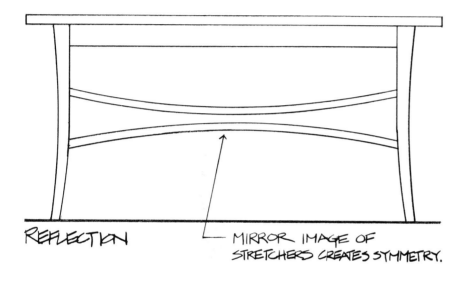

REFLECTION — MIRROR IMAGE OF STRETCHERS CREATES SYMMETRY.

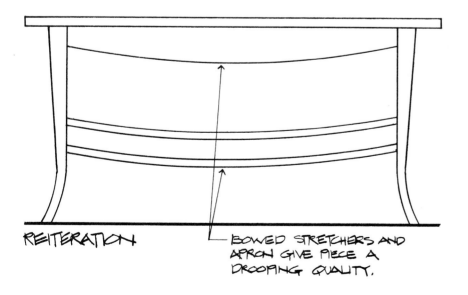

REITERATION — BOWED STRETCHERS AND APRON GIVE PIECE A DROOPING QUALITY.

visual tension Visual tension is an element of the visual vocabulary often used to create compositional interest. Composing what appears to be a physically unstable or precarious situation or implying some sort of physical stress in materials or between forms can add greatly to the interest a piece generates. Each element in a composition may have a form or edge that works well with another element in a dynamic way. For example, the stretchers of the table in the drawing below left create visual tension because the points at the edges of the circular forms almost—but not quite—touch. If there were more distance between the stretchers or if they touched, visual tension would be eliminated. If

The backs of these chairs by Frank Nadel of Basalt, Colo., generate visual tension because the two halves don't quite touch. Separate the forms a little more and tension would be reduced; join the halves and tension would be eliminated. (Photo by Dean Powell.)

VISUAL TENSION IN A COMPOSITION

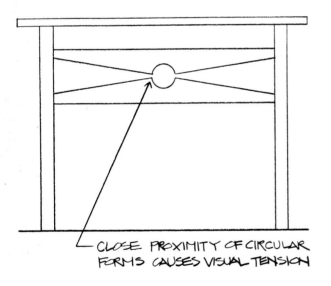

CLOSE PROXIMITY OF CIRCULAR FORMS CAUSES VISUAL TENSION

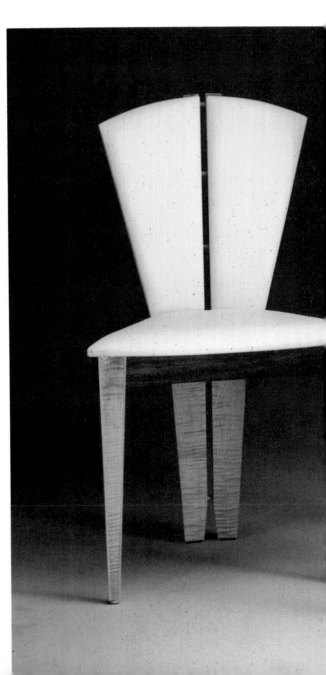

two forms are close to touching, there is usually a shadowline between them that helps define their separation. (If this shadowline does not exist, you can create a background, perhaps a darkened line or color change, to emphasize the separation.)

Color can also influence tension, and a color change at the edge of forms in tension can sometimes intensify the effect. Complementary colors (see p. 111) naturally promote tension because they are opposites on the color wheel and have an energizing effect when used together.

Certain situations call for actual, not implied, physical tension (for instance, when wood is bent through the use of tensioning cables and turnbuckles), but

these may or may not visually suggest tension. The eye discerns whether a material is manipulated in a natural way (such as a piece of wood bent from pressure exerted on one end) or whether it is formed into shape (as a bentwood scroll, or a reverse curve, such as used in the bentwood furniture of the 1800s). In either situation, if the form or composition of a piece makes it appear that it is being restrained and might spring back or that pressure is being exerted or that forces are acting on the material, then visual tension will exist.

proportioning a piece

Proportion is a fundamental issue in furniture design. Subtle changes in proportion produce substantial changes in a piece and determine whether it is graceful or awkward. All other efforts in design and detailing are in vain if the proportions of a piece are not right.

Proportions are either relative or absolute. Relative proportion is the size of one object in relation to another, and indeed in relation to a room. It becomes especially important in the design of complementary pieces, such as a matching desk and chair, where each piece must be in proportion to the other piece in addition to being well proportioned within itself. Absolute proportion is defined as the relation of an object to itself, for example, the proportion of one side to another in a chest.

To understand how proportion differs from scale (p. 75), consider a suite of dollhouse furniture in which all the pieces complement each other as well as being attractive in themselves. We could easily talk about the relative and absolute proportion of these pieces. But if we were to compare these miniatures to a suite of full-scale furniture intended for the great hall of a castle, for instance, we would have to discuss their scale, that is, the overall impact of their smallness or largeness to the viewer's eye. In this case, we would speak of the scale of the doll-

LEFT: The absolute proportion of this American teakettle stand (1775-1800) is not very appealing because the base is too heavy and too wide for the small top. (Photo courtesy Museum of Art, Rhode Island School of Design.)

FACING PAGE: This tea table works well, because all the elements are in pleasing proportion. (Photo courtesy Museum of Art, Rhode Island School of Design, bequest of Charles L. Pendleton.)

This wardrobe by Todd Smith of Califon, N.J., is a good example of a well-proportioned piece of furniture. (Photo by Commercial Photography.)

house furniture as tiny, while the scale of the castle suite would appear massive.

How are proportions established? Sometimes they are suggested by function or space limitations, but when there are no given restraints, pleasing proportions can initially be arrived at through formulas. Some of these follow. It's interesting to note that proportioning systems were originally developed by architects in search of visual order. Because buildings are generally large in scale and only one facade is seen at a time, architectural proportion was developed two dimensionally. Historically, furniture proportions were determined the same way. Since they were to be viewed frontally, however, many pieces were designed with a prominent facade—the back and sides were considered secondary. This worked well for secretaries and chests of drawers, which were usually pushed against a wall. But because furniture is usually so much smaller than architecture, it's often seen in the round, and the entire form should be appealing from every view.

Good proportion can therefore be achieved only when the entire piece is considered—the proportion of the front to the side, for instance, as well as the proportions of the front within itself. Remember, any proportioning system should be used only as a starting point for making design decisions. Design is not an exercise in geometry. There really isn't any right or wrong system for any given problem, and there is no system that by itself can solve all proportioning problems.

In addition, factors such as composition, detailing, structure, texture and color can affect the proportion of a piece by changing what the eye most readily perceives. This distortion can be used to advantage by a designer when basic proportion is dictated by function or space requirements, because it allows what might be an unpleasing proportion to be visually altered. Look at the drawings on the facing page to see how the introduction of some other elements can affect the perception of proportion.

some proportioning systems

the golden section   Probably the best known and most widely used proportioning system is the golden section, which seems to satisfy our sense of harmony better than any other. The basis of the golden section is that a division of a length or a shape is such that the smaller is to the greater as the greater is to the whole. In the drawing on p. 96, line B-C is to line A-B as line A-B is to line A-C. This ratio is 1:1.618, approximately 5 to 8. For example, if line A-C is 15.6 in., line A-B can be determined by dividing 15.6 in. by 1.618, equalling 9.64 in. Line B-C would then equal 5.96 in. Likewise, if you know the

AN EXERCISE IN PROPORTIONING

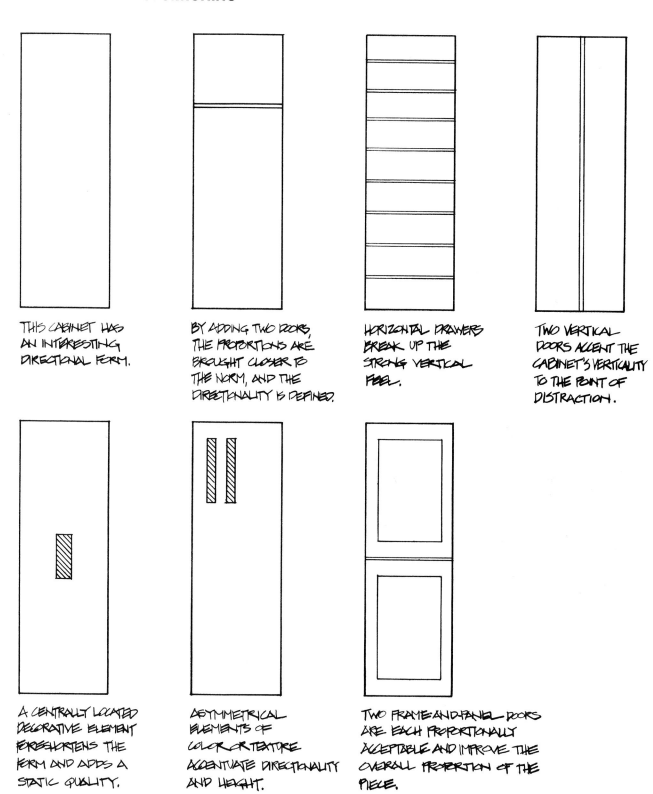

THIS CABINET HAS AN INTERESTING DIRECTIONAL FORM.

BY ADDING TWO DOORS, THE PROPORTIONS ARE BROUGHT CLOSER TO THE NORM, AND THE DIRECTIONALITY IS DEFINED.

HORIZONTAL DRAWERS BREAK UP THE STRONG VERTICAL FEEL.

TWO VERTICAL DOORS ACCENT THE CABINET'S VERTICALITY TO THE POINT OF DISTRACTION.

A CENTRALLY LOCATED DECORATIVE ELEMENT FORESHORTENS THE FORM AND ADDS A STATIC QUALITY.

ASYMMETRICAL ELEMENTS OF COLOR OR TEXTURE ACCENTUATE DIRECTIONALITY AND HEIGHT.

TWO FRAME AND PANEL DOORS ARE EACH PROPORTIONALLY ACCEPTABLE AND IMPROVE THE OVERALL PROPORTION OF THE PIECE.

THE GOLDEN SECTION

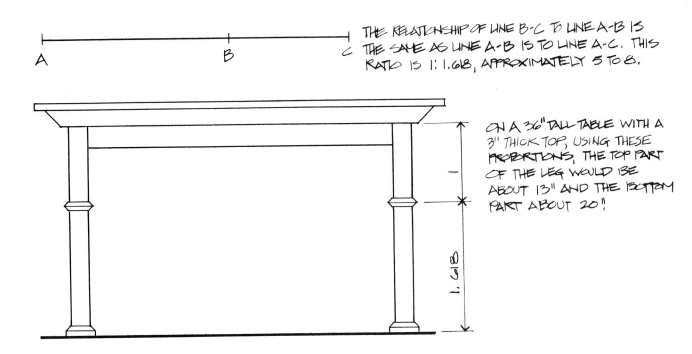

THE RELATIONSHIP OF LINE B-C TO LINE A-B IS THE SAME AS LINE A-B IS TO LINE A-C. THIS RATIO IS 1:1.618, APPROXIMATELY 5 TO 8.

ON A 36" TALL TABLE WITH A 3" THICK TOP, USING THESE PROPORTIONS, THE TOP PART OF THE LEG WOULD BE ABOUT 13" AND THE BOTTOM PART ABOUT 20"!

length of line B-C, multiplying it by 1.618 will give the length of line A-B.

The golden section is found quite often in nature as well as in manmade objects over the centuries. Used in furniture, it can help develop both the overall form and detail form of a piece. The table shown in the drawing on the facing page uses the golden section as its proportioning basis.

the golden rectangle The golden rectangle comes from the golden section; in the drawing at right, the ratio of side A to side B is 1:1.618. A golden rectangle can easily be constructed by drawing a square of any size and bisecting side AB to create point E, as shown. Using E-C as a radius, swing an arc as shown, and locate point F at the intersection of the arc and the extension of line A-B. Draw a perpendicular from F and locate point G where it intersects the extension of line D-C to complete the golden rectangle AFGD. By continually subdividing the golden rectangle into squares and smaller golden rectangles, a spiral can be constructed. (Logarithmic variants on this spiral are frequently found in nature; for example, in the shells of various mollusks.) The proportions of the buffet in the photo on the facing page are based on the golden rectangle; each prominent rectangular element on its face has a proportional basis of 1:1.618.

geometric progression This is a progression in which each unit increases by a constant ratio, for example, 1, 2, 4, 8, etc., or 1, 3, 9, 27, etc. In geometric progression, the ratio of consecutive units is the same—the first unit is to the second unit as the second unit is to the third, and so on. You can use this system in a furniture piece to proportion forms (such as a chest and its drawers), details (such as the relationship of molding sizes in a piece), or the spacing of parts (such as stretchers in a table). The drawing on p. 98 shows how geometric progression can be used to articulate the form of a table leg or to proportion a sideboard with a stepped front.

arithmetic progression In arithmetic progression, there is a constant difference between consecutive units in the series, for example, 3, 5, 7, 9 or 5, 10,

Gerrit Rietveld's 1919 beechwood buffet is based on the golden rectangle. The sides of each major rectangular element on its face have a proportional relationship of 1:1.618. (Photo courtesy Barry Friedman Ltd., New York, N.Y.)

CONSTRUCTING A GOLDEN RECTANGLE

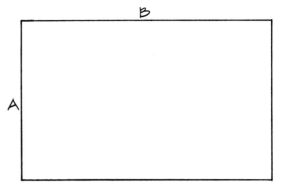

THE GOLDEN RECTANGLE IS DERIVED FROM THE GOLDEN SECTION. THE RATIO OF SIDE A TO SIDE B IS 1:1.618.

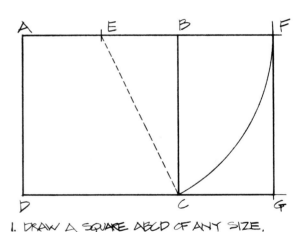

1. DRAW A SQUARE ABCD OF ANY SIZE.
2. BISECT SIDE AB TO CREATE POINT E.
3. USING EC AS A RADIUS, SWING AN ARC TO LOCATE POINT F.
4. DRAW IN LINES B-F, F-G AND C-G.
5. THE RESULT IS GOLDEN RECTANGLE AFGD.

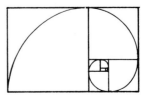

BY CONTINUALLY SUBDIVIDING A GOLDEN RECTANGLE INTO SQUARES AND SMALLER GOLDEN RECTANGLES, A SPIRAL CAN BE CREATED.

GEOMETRIC PROGRESSION

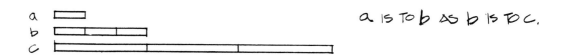

a

b

c

a is to b as b is to c.

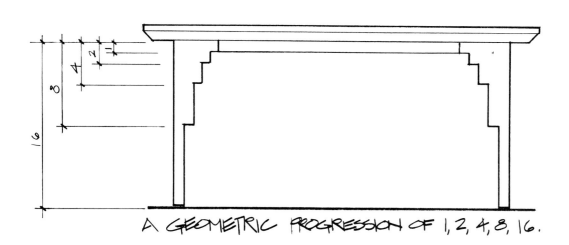

A GEOMETRIC PROGRESSION OF 1, 2, 4, 8, 16.

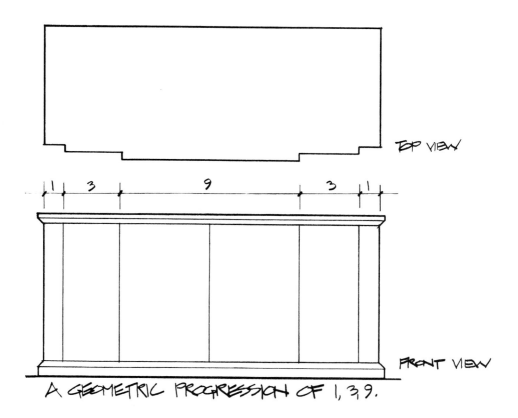

TOP VIEW

FRONT VIEW

A GEOMETRIC PROGRESSION OF 1, 3, 9.

15, 20. In furniture design, this system has useful applications in the spacing of parts or in graduating multiples of parts (such as drawers in a chest). Arithmetic progression is also helpful in proportioning elements such as the length and width of a chair seat in relation to the width and height of its back. An arithmetic system is especially useful in modular furniture, where the proportionate size increase of a part is consistent (meaning that the size increase of each part is the same as the previous increase). The drawing below shows how the system of arithmetic progression might be applied in the design of a table leg or chest of drawers.

ARITHMETIC PROGRESSION

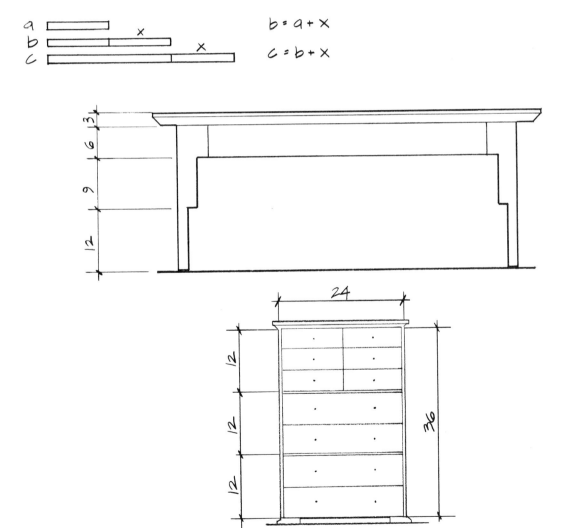

harmonic progression In harmonic progression, the reciprocals of the units form an arithmetic progression, such as $1/3$, $1/5$, $1/7$, $1/9$ or $1/1$, $1/4$, $1/7$, $1/10$. (The reciprocal of any unit is obtained by dividing it into 1—the reciprocal of 4 is $1/4$.) In the drawing below, the progression is $1/2$, $1/3$, $1/4$, $1/5$, $1/6$. If A equals 60 in., the progression will be as follows:

B ($1/2$) = 30 in.
C ($1/3$) = 20 in.
D ($1/4$) = 15 in.
E ($1/5$) = 12 in.
F ($1/6$) = 10 in.

HARMONIC PROGRESSION

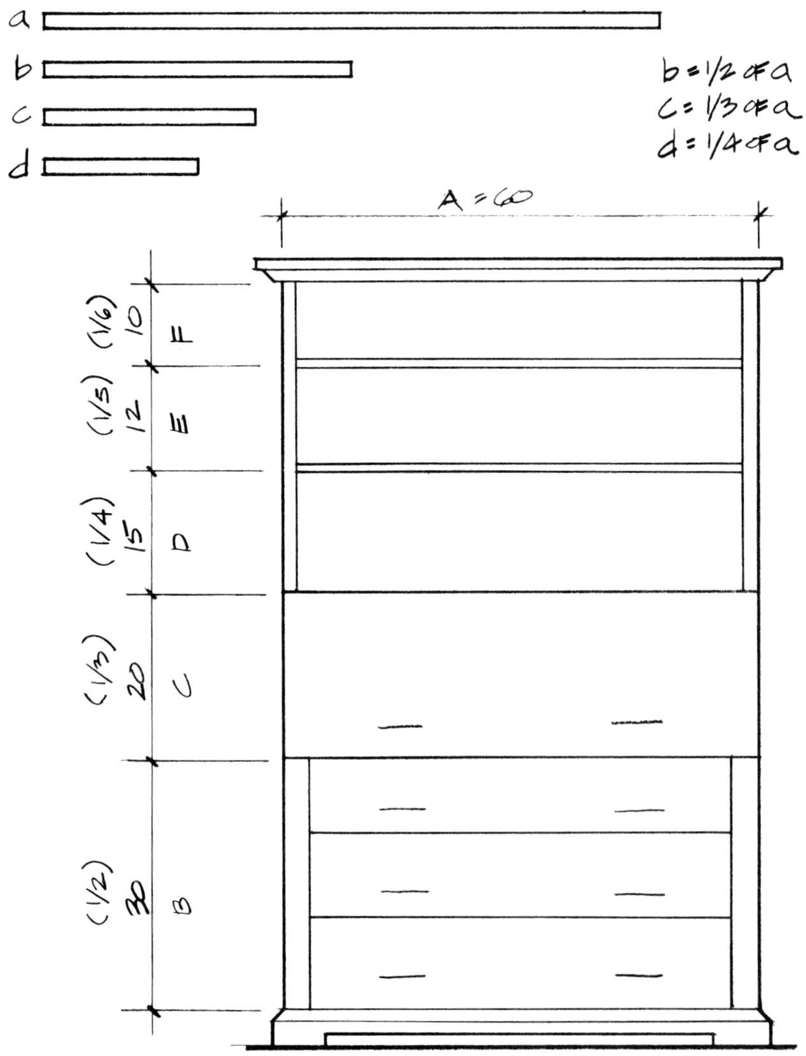
a
b
c
d
b=1/2 of a
c=1/3 of a
d=1/4 of a
A=60
(1/6) 10 F
(1/5) 12 E
(1/4) 15 D
(1/3) 20 C
(1/2) 30 B

Proportioning by harmonic progression works in furniture where a gradually decreasing spacing or sizing of elements is desired. The drawing on the facing page shows how this system could be used in a secretary.

Fibonacci series   In the Fibonacci series, each unit is the sum of the preceding two: 1, 1, 2, 3, 5, 8, 13, etc. As the series progresses, the ratio of consecutive units approaches the golden-section relationship, that is, 1:1.618. Like harmonic progression, this system is helpful where a gradation of sizes is desired. The drawing below shows how it could be used in the design of a table leg or chest.

the five orders of classical architecture   This architectural proportioning method is used in the design of various styles of columns. It has some application to the design of furniture, especially if the

FIBONACCI SERIES

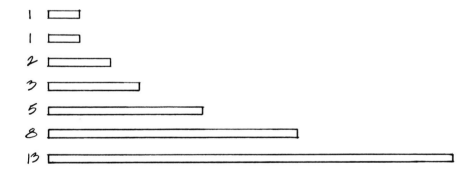

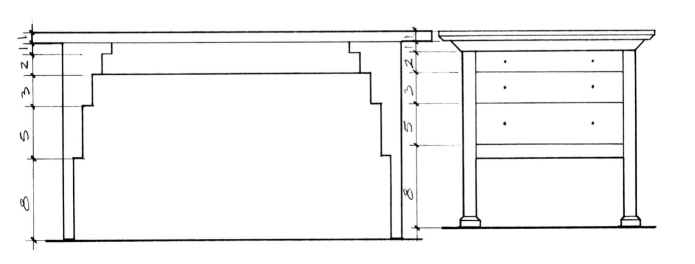

piece has columnar elements. The five orders, as described by Vitruvius, a first-century Roman architect, and revived by Thomas Chippendale, a famous English furniture maker (1718-1779), are Tuscan, Doric, Ionic, Corinthian and Composite. The height of each order is divided into five equal parts, one of which is the height of the pedestal; the others are collectively subdivided into various other units which are further subdivided in various ways, depending on the order. See Chippendale's book, listed in the Bibliography (pp. 212-213), for specifics.

the anthropomorphic system The anthropomorphic system is based on the dimensional relationships of parts of the human body to the whole, because a well-shaped human body is considered to be well balanced proportionally. Vitruvius made some of these proportional observations. He discovered that the forearm and breadth of the breast are one-fourth of the height of the body. The foot is one-sixth, the head from the chin to the crown is one-eighth and the open hand from the tip of the middle finger to the wrist is one-tenth total height. Other parts of the body, such as the face, have proportional relationships within themselves.

The navel is considered to be the center point in the front view of a man or woman—if the total height of the human body from the feet to the hand of a vertically raised arm is divided into two equal parts, the division will occur at the navel. If a horizontal line is drawn through the average man or woman at this point, it will be approximately ⅝ of the person's total height, which is very close to the golden-section ratio of 1:1.618. Le Corbusier, a French architect, also used these observations to create his Modulor, which was a set of scales derived from the primary proportions and dimensions of the body. These scales helped him design objects, furniture included, whose proportions would be sympathetic to human proportions. The relationships of adjacent parts of the human body correspond closely to the golden section, and the proportioning of a linear form or width-to-height ratio can be set up from this relationship in the same manner.

Hambidge (root) rectangles Hambidge rectangles are generated geometrically from a square. They are called root rectangles because the length of each successive rectangle is calculated by taking the square root of the sum of squared width plus squared length (i.e., the diagonal) of the previous square or rectangle. They result in the successive ratios of widths to lengths of 1:1.41, 1:1.73, 1:2, 1:2.23, etc., because the first rectangle length generated is the square root of two (1.41), the second length the

HAMBIDGE RECTANGLES

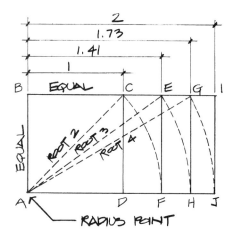

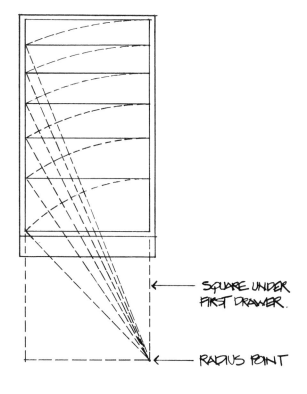

square root of 3 (1.73), etc. This system, first used by the ancient Greeks and revived by the American scholar Jay Hambidge, can be especially helpful in working out a set of graduated drawers in a chest.

The drawing on the facing page shows a drafting method for constructing Hambidge rectangles, which produces a smooth gradation of forms. Start with a square. Draw a diagonal line from one corner of the square (point A) to another (point C). Next, create point F by placing the point of a compass on A and drawing an arc from point C until it intersects with an extension of line A-D. Then draw in the lines C-E and E-F to complete the first rectangle.

Now draw a diagonal across rectangle ABEF (line A-E) and, keeping the radius point at A, strike another arc to intersect with an extension of line A-D at point H. Draw in the remaining sides to complete the rectangle ABGH. Repeat this procedure with successive diagonals and rectangles until the desired number of graduations is reached.

To proportion graduated drawers in a chest, start by drawing in a square directly underneath the lower drawer in the front view, as shown in the drawing. Remember that the height of each gradation is a function of the size of the initial square, so the overall height of the chest is determined by the number of gradations included. If a specific height is desired, you may have to experiment with the width of the chest (because the width determines the size of the initial square, which in turn determines the height of each gradation). The formula and chart at right, calculated by a mathematician friend of mine, can be used to proportion a graduated chest of drawers if either the height or the width is known. The formula is $H = N \times W$, where H = height of chest, W = width of chest, and N = ratio value given to the number of drawers in a chest.

Suppose we want a chest 60 in. high (minus the kickplate height) with five drawers. What width gives us the proportion dictated by the Hambidge rectangles? Using the ratio table, you can see the N-value for a chest with five drawers is 1.449. Solving the equation for W (W = 60 in. ÷ 1.449), we get a width of 41.41 in.

A well-proportioned piece In the table on p. 104, the overall proportions as well as the proportions of some of the parts are roughly based on the golden section—the drawing on p. 105 shows the relationships. The height/width ratio of the piece approximates the golden-section ratio of 1:1.618, as does the foot detail. The ¾-in. dimension at the bottom of the leg is to the 1¼-in. dimension of the widest part of the foot (ratio 1:1.66), as the 1¼-in. dimension is to the 2-in. height of the foot (ratio

n-value chart

N-value is the ratio between the height and width of the Hambidge-rectangle progression for a chest of drawers.

N-value depends on the number of drawers in a chest; this table gives the value for 1 to 15 drawers.

number of drawers in chest	n-value	number of drawers in chest	n-value
1	.414	9	2.162
2	.732	10	2.317
3	1.000	11	2.464
4	1.236	12	2.606
5	1.449	13	2.742
6	1.646	14	2.873
7	1.828	15	3.000
8	2.000		

1:1.60). To avoid the predictability that could have resulted from using just one proportioning system, the apron and the edging of the table are based on the arithmetic progression of 1, 2, 3. The edging around the tabletop and the bevels above and below it are of equal ⅜-in. widths, as shown in the detail. The apron width is also composed of straight and curved parts, each based on a 2-in. dimension. If each dimension of either the edging or the apron were added to the next, the progression would be constant. (The edging progression would be ⅜ in.,

This table by John Dunnigan of West Kingston, R.I., uses the golden rectangle as the basis for its major proportion (see the drawing on the facing page). For variety, Dunnigan relied on an arithmetic proportion for some of the table's details. (Photo by Roger Birn.)

¾ in., 1⅛ in., and the apron 2 in., 4 in., 6 in. Dividing by the lowest common denominator would give the progression of 1, 2, 3 in each case.)

In this same table, an interesting proportional reversal contributes to the overall balance of the piece. The proportional balance of mass (heavy on the top, light on the bottom) is reversed in the proportional balance of color (light line of color on the top, more concentrated area of color in the feet.) There really isn't a system to create this kind of relationship—it is simply a matter of good aesthetic judgment.

PROPORTIONING SYSTEMS IN A TABLE

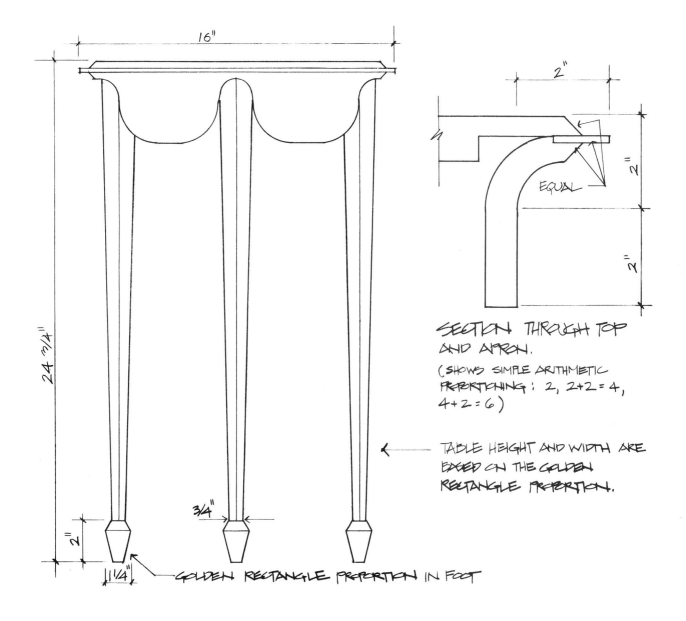

SECTION THROUGH TOP
AND APRON.
(SHOWS SIMPLE ARITHMETIC
PROPORTIONING: 2, 2+2=4,
4+2=6)

TABLE HEIGHT AND WIDTH ARE
BASED ON THE GOLDEN
RECTANGLE PROPORTION.

GOLDEN RECTANGLE PROPORTION IN FOOT

color, texture and ornamentation

In this chapter we'll look at the elements of the visual vocabulary that deal with the surface treatment of furniture. The surface of any material used in furniture construction can be painted, textured, silk-screened, ornamented, distressed or any combination of these or other processes. Sometimes the entire concept of a piece is based on one of these elements. Other times these elements are regarded as an afterthought. But leaving surface treatment to the last minute is always a mistake, as its effect on a piece can be monumental.

some principles of color use

As the photos on the facing page show, color can completely alter the mood of a piece. Change the color of a chair from somber black to bright yellow and you will totally change its character. Construct a box in padauk instead of mahogany and you will create such a powerful richness of color that it may become more important than the box itself. Color undeniably calls attention to itself and to whatever it touches. A revival of painted surfaces in the early 1980s by furniture designers and craftsmen has created limitless possibilities for color use. Certainly the use of color in furniture is not new. Polychromy, which is the embellishment of furniture with multi-colored paint, is an ancient means of decoration. And color and pattern in the form of upholstery have traditionally been used to adorn and enhance wooden furniture.

Two loveseats by Mitch Ryerson of Cambridge, Mass., show how color can dramatically change the character of a piece of furniture. The use of two hues of strong intensity gives the deep-blue piece (top photo) a luxurious, formal feel; red, which defines the edges, is the dominant color. The same loveseat takes on a more casual mood in medium blue (bottom photo); here color also accents the outline of the piece. (Top photo by Dean Powell; bottom photo by Mitch Ryerson.)

rudimentary color theory   In order to use color thoughtfully in furniture design, it's first necessary to know something about color theory. White light consists of all the colors of the spectrum, each having a different frequency. When the light waves of all frequencies are reflected by an object, the object appears white. When the light waves of all frequencies are absorbed, the object appears black. Color occurs when some of the waves are absorbed and some are reflected.

The colors of the spectrum fall within three divisions: primary colors, secondary colors and tertiary colors. A color wheel, a device to organize the color spectrum, can be a great help in choosing the colors of paints and materials for furniture, as we will see later. A color wheel is shown in the drawing on the facing page. Here is how it works.

The primary colors of red, blue and yellow are spaced at equal intervals around the wheel. Mixing them together forms the secondary colors: red + yellow = orange; yellow + blue = green; blue + red = violet. On the color wheel, the secondary colors are located midway between the primaries. Mixing adjoining primary and secondary colors forms the tertiary colors, shown as wedges in the drawing, which complete the twelve-part wheel. Yellow + orange = yellow-orange; red + orange = red-orange; red + violet = red-violet; blue + violet = blue-violet; blue + green = blue-green; yellow + green = yellow-green. The sequence of colors depicted in the color wheel is the natural color spectrum, as you would see in a rainbow. Colors that are opposite each other in the wheel are called complementary colors.

Colors can be further classified according to the characteristics of hue, intensity and value. Hue, the dominant identifying factor, distinguishes one color from another, such as red from green. Hues can be warm (red, orange and yellow) or cool (blue, green and violet). Hue has a great psychological impact on a viewer because it can evoke associations and create a mood. Red is exciting and attention-grabbing; blue is cool and serene. Warmth and cheerfulness are associated with yellow and orange; green is usually considered restful. The warmth of a color can even overpower the coolness of a material—imagine a steel-frame stool painted bright red.

Intensity (also called chroma) refers to the saturation of a hue with color, or how pure the hue appears as opposed to how much greyness is in it. An intense color is one that approaches a pure hue, while a dull color is one that approaches neutral grey (a grey halfway between black and white). Orange, violet and royal blue are intense colors. Tan, rose, sea green and slate blue are dull colors.

Using a color wheel is a good way to organize the color spectrum.

COLOR WHEEL

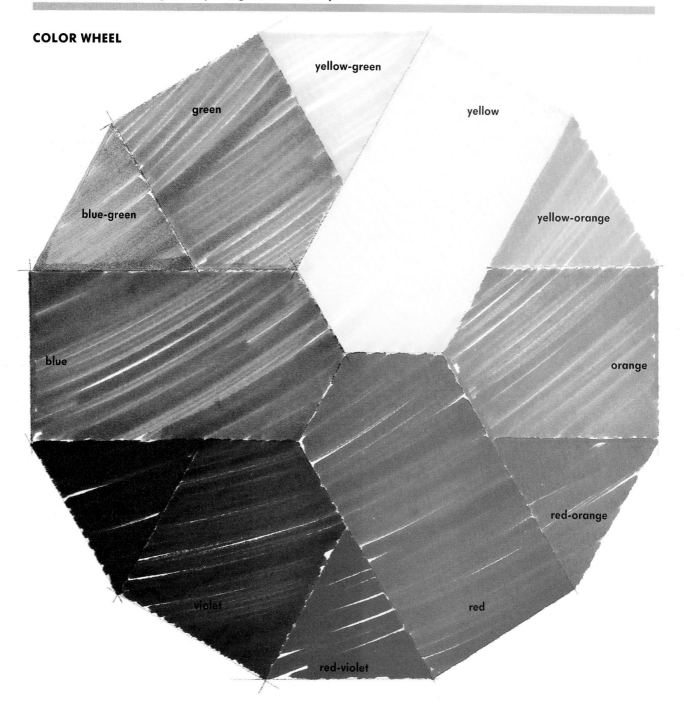

yellow-green

yellow

green

blue-green

yellow-orange

blue

orange

violet

red-orange

red

red-violet

Value refers to the brilliancy (brightness) or lightness of a color. It is gauged on a scale of greys between white and black. Colors that appear dark, such as maroon or forest green, are low in value. Colors that appear bright, such as lemon yellow or sky blue, are considered high in value. The value of a color can be increased by the addition of white, after which the color is called a tint (pink, peach, lavender). If black or a darker color of the same hue is mixed with a color, the value of the color decreases, and the color is called a shade (brown, olive, navy).

approaches to color organization Although harmony among colors in furniture is not always desirable, a harmonious palette is a good way to begin to experiment with color. Here are three systems of color organization.

BELOW: Monochromatic color schemes can create harmony in furniture, as illustrated by these lacquered Imperial Chests by Shiro Kuramata of Japan. (Photo courtesy Grace Designs, Dallas, Tex.)

FACING PAGE: Cloud Table by Everett Bramhall of Cambridge, Mass., explores how complementary colors can interact to create a mood of high energy. (Photo by Seth Stem.)

In the monochromatic approach, one color is varied by using different values and intensities. A monochromatic color scheme can be quite striking if an interesting hue is chosen, and if in part of the monochromatic range the hue is high in value and intensity. For instance, if blue were selected as the basic hue for the piece, the palette could include a royal blue, which is of high intensity; a sky blue, which is high in value; and a navy blue, which is relatively dull. Used sensitively, this color scheme can have a great deal of visual impact. However, if you want a visually forceful design but choose a relatively neutral or dull color, other design elements may have to be enlisted to generate dynamism. The visual appeal of the chests on the facing page, for example, comes from their long, simple legs and tamboured fronts, not from their grey color.

Another option is to use complementary colors. The color chart at right shows the different relationships. A direct relationship, indicated by the red arrows on the chart, is when two colors opposite each other in the wheel are used. A split complementary relationship, indicated by the black triangle, consists of three colors, two of which are on either side of the color opposite the first one. A triadic relationship, indicated by the blue triangle, occurs when three colors spaced equally around the wheel are used. Two direct complementary colors, orange and blue, were used on the table in the photo below. The intensity and value of the colors are high, and relationships are made even stronger because the colors are airbrushed adjacent to areas of black.

COMPLEMENTARY COLORS

The red arrows in the diagram below show direct complements. The black triangle shows a split complementary group. The blue triangle shows a triadic harmony group. Rotate the symbols to any position on the circle to locate similar color relationships.

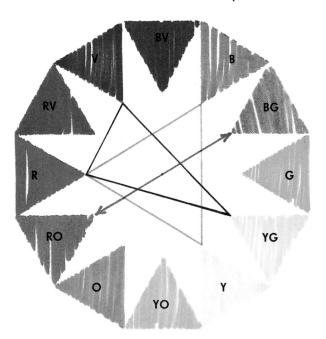

ANALOGOUS COLORS

Here is an arbitrary selection of analogous colors. Groups of varying sizes are each balanced on a primary color. Analogous groupings can be selected from any segment of the circle and can be limited to as few as two colors.

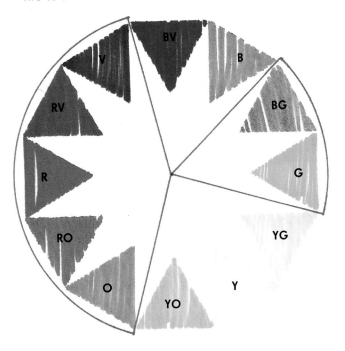

The analogous approach uses colors that are adjacent to each other on the wheel. As shown in the drawing at left, group size can vary, with as few as two colors in a group, but each group is balanced on a primary color. In an analogous combination, one color can be dominant and the adjacent ones used to balance it. In this manner, subtle gradations are achieved, perhaps implying change or evolution.

selecting and using the palette   In addition to the above systems of color organization, there are as many intuitive ways to select colors as there are furniture designers. How a professional designer selects colors depends on his or her role in the field. An interior designer may turn to industry forecasts to project what colors are likely to be "in." A contract-furniture designer might select neutral colors that will complement a variety of interiors, so the pieces will appeal to a broad cross section of clients. Furniture designers who do speculative, limited editions or one-offs have the luxury of using color any way they choose, even in shocking or clashing arrangements. Commissioned furniture, on the other hand, usually has to suit the color sensibility of the client. Here are some guidelines for choosing colors.

Everyone is partial to a particular color spectrum, but here again, a designer should seek to identify the colors that best support the concept of the piece. Otherwise design opportunities may be restricted, and the impact of the work will be diminished. A

piece of furniture designed to have a feeling of extreme mass, for instance, could be diminished by the use of pearwood and pastels instead of rosewood and dull colors.

In painting a piece with multiple colors, one color is usually chosen as dominant, or one should appear in the background and another in the foreground. However, while the background color is essentially the major color in the piece, it is not necessarily the dominant color, for both warmth and intensity dictate whether a color will recede toward the background or advance toward the viewer. For example, in the photo below, you can see that the orange pattern, which is warm and intense, seems to advance

FACING PAGE: The analogous colors of yellow, orange and yellow-green were used in this lacquered table by Everett Bramhall of Cambridge, Mass. (Photo by Everett Bramhall.)

BELOW: The orange pattern advances toward the viewer while the green background recedes in this table by Mark Lorah, of Providence, R.I. This occurs because warm colors dominate cool colors. (Photo by Seth Stem.)

over the overall green background, which is cooler and lighter in value.

How intense a color appears is relative to the intensity of the colors it is used with. For example, an orange drawer pull on a pale-yellow drawer front will appear more intense than the same orange pull on a red drawer front. (The value of a color is also relative—a light color will appear lighter against a dark background.)

The circumstances under which a color will be viewed will also affect a viewer's perception. For example, a warm color will usually appear warmer when contrasted with a cool color—a red painted on a light blue surface will appear warmer than the same red painted on a bright orange surface. Likewise, a bright red cedar chest in a pine-paneled room will look warm; in a room with white walls, it will appear blazing.

The balance of color temperatures is one of the first things that I consider in designing a piece, whether I am planning to use natural materials or painted surfaces. Wood in its natural state is warm not only because of its grain but also because of its color. Both dark woods such as walnut and Honduras mahogany and light woods such as ash and maple are warm because of their reddish-brown and yellowish hues, respectively. The walnut and mahogany appear warmer because their colors are more intense than those of maple and ash.

Fortunately, most types of wood can be used together because the common hues of yellow, brown, red, orange and purple relate well. But when wood and fabric or paint are combined, it's easy to run into trouble. For example, I once made a closet storage unit having cloth-covered panels surrounded by red oak frames. For this unit, I first selected a brown twill that I was sure would go well with the yellowish red of the oak. I was mistaken, however, because the brown of the fabric was on the cool side, and the background of the twill, which was faintly visible, was cool white. The warmth of the wood just didn't work well with the coolness of the fabric. I next selected a medium-warm grey fabric, which worked fine not only because both colors were warm but also because the neutral grey complemented the yellowish oak. As another example, you wouldn't choose fire-engine red upholstery to go with cherry, because the combination would look brash. Better choices for cherry would be cream or greyish-green turquoise.

As with most issues in design, a woodworker's first experiments with color, whether natural or applied, should start simply. For example, choose one color as a background and then add others as accents. (It's a sure bet that a beginner using different

colors in equal amounts will create visual conflict, especially when using woods of closely related hues, intensities and values.) Use the second color to enhance the piece's detailing—to emphasize edges, the ends of legs, areas of molding or a recess. Or use the second color to create an entirely new detail or an overall pattern on top of the background color. Use a small pattern if the forms of the piece are complicated. Try to assign colors logically, but leave at least a little room for intrigue. The table on the facing page, for example, uses a purely logical approach, incorporating color to separate the elements of the piece. The problem is that there is no dominant color, and the piece suffers from lack of visual interest overall. In contrast, the table below uses color in a way that is just as logical but much more intriguing. Here the contrasting wood inlay is in no way related to the separation of structural elements, but creates a decorative pattern all its own.

FACING PAGE: There is a close balance of natural wood colors in this table by Robert LeBlanc of Providence, R.I., so no one color has clear dominance. This perfectly logical arrangement results in a bland look. (Photo by Seth Stem.)

BELOW: This hall table by John Everdell of Cambridge, Mass., uses color for unity by threading a similar element throughout the design. (Photo by Susie Cushner.)

Painted surfaces can have incredibly different characters. A chair painted in bright, poster-paint colors can easily take on a manufactured look; a chair colored with milk paint will have an heirloom feeling. Likewise, a sprayed-on color might have a colder feel than a brushed color if you can see tiny brush strokes on the surface. Remember, however, that the glossiness of the finish will affect color perception. A glossy finish causes glare, which is a barrier to color. Matte finishes allow better perception of hue and intensity as well as the possibility of tex-

LEFT: Color calls attention to the drawer pulls and door latch of this telephone cabinet by Rosanne Somerson, of Westport, Mass. The outside of the piece is composed of closely related pastels. When the cabinet door is opened, a bright raspberry surface provides a pleasant surprise. (Photo by Dean Powell.)

BELOW LEFT: A rich color palette enlivens Ménage à Trois by Mitch Ryerson of Cambridge, Mass. Color here is used to separate structural elements in the bench and to call attention to forms. (Photo by Dean Powell.)

ture being used with the color (see the discussion of texture below). Matte surfaces recede into the material, and glossy finishes jump back at the viewer.

As a last note, when developing a color palette, be sure to research the toxic properties of the paint, as well as its aging qualities. For example, sign-painter's paint, which comes in beautiful rich colors, contains lead and would therefore be inappropriate for use on children's furniture. Aniline dyes tend to fade over the years. Most commercial house paints, which are often used on furniture, have a life expectancy of less than 15 years.

the role of texture in furniture

Altering a surface from smooth to textured will change both the character and the light-reflective quality of the material. Too often materials, especially wood, are visualized only in a highly refined or finished state. Often, however, furniture can benefit from texture as a design element. As shown in the drawing, texture can enhance a piece in many ways. It adds contrast and interest, and even alters the way proportion is perceived. Texture calls attention to detailing or makes a functional element more visually dominant. It can separate or define elements, areas and forms, and create imagery.

Many materials readily accept textural manipulation because their surfaces are inherently bland. Paper, sheet aluminum and glass are examples. It's easy

TEXTURE CAN BE USED TO SEPARATE OR DEFINE ELEMENTS,

...OR TO CREATE IMAGERY.

THE USES OF TEXTURE IN FURNITURE

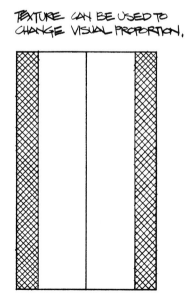

TEXTURE CAN BE USED TO CHANGE VISUAL PROPORTION.

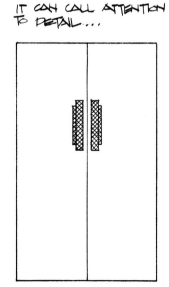

IT CAN CALL ATTENTION TO DETAIL...

...OR DEFINE THE ENDING OF A FURNITURE ELEMENT.

to introduce visual activity by embossing or drawing on paper; sandblasting or cutting glass; and grinding, hammering or stippling aluminum. Wood is in a different category because its surface has natural beauty. If wood is textured, its grain patterns are obscured. Despite this drawback, a case can be made for texturing rather than painting a pattern on wood, because while the warmth of the wood is maintained in a textured state, if the wood is painted, the natural warmth is completely lost.

The methods and means of texturing a surface are virtually limitless. I have seen cabinets lined with

BELOW: Everett Bramhall of Cambridge, Mass., created a texture on the edge of the top and a pattern on the base of Mamumba Table by burning the wood with hot branding irons. (Photo by Seth Stem.)

FACING PAGE, LEFT: The texture on the edge of this 18th-century card table visually reduces the thickness of the top. (Photo courtesy Museum of Art, Rhode Island School of Design, bequest of Charles L. Pendleton.)

FACING PAGE, RIGHT: The texture of this chest by Michael Hurwitz, of Philadelphia, Pa., was developed by bandsawing the lumber with an antiquated bandsaw. The wood was covered with paint, which was rubbed off before it dried, a process that accentuated the ridges and valleys left by the saw. (Photo by Tom Brummett.)

long-haired fur (intriguing to some, bizarre to others) and aluminum desk bases patterned with a grinding disk. The pieces shown here illustrate a few other approaches. In the mahogany table in the photo on the facing page, a recessed black pattern of texture was applied to the table edges and base with branding irons, which were fabricated by cutting out patterns in steel and welding them to a backing structure and handle. The branding irons were heated red-hot in a forge, then pressed against the surface of the wood. The designer chose the branding process because the markings complemented the African character intended for the piece, and because the rich, brownish-black color of the brands complemented the mahogany.

To create a primitive feeling, the wood of the chest shown in the photo at right was left just as it came off the antiquated bandsaw (with an inaccurate blade-tracking system) that was used to cut it. To accentuate the machined texture, the piece was then painted and the paint immediately wiped off, removing the color from the ridges but leaving it in the recesses.

The double top of the 18th-century card table shown in the photo below unfolds to a single thickness; texture on the table edge visually reduces the thickness when the top is folded by breaking up the plain surface. But texture need not be a surface development—for example, it can even come from the repetitive use of small three-dimensional forms under a glass-top table.

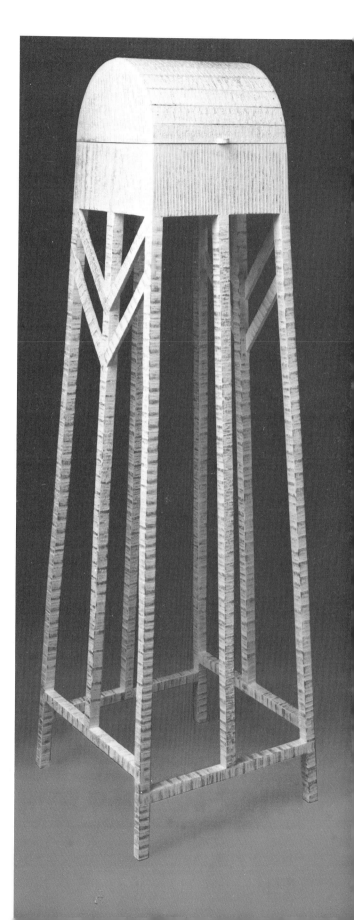

ornamentation

Ornamentation refers to the decoration or embellishment of an object to add to its beauty or give it meaning or importance. Because ornamentation is not necessarily connected to the structure or mechanics of a piece, there are limitless expressive possibilities, including the incorporation of stained glass and carved, inlaid or molded wood, as well as silk screening and stenciling. Ornamentation can be as primitive as nailing decorative wrought-iron hinges onto the doors of a Spanish-style cabinet or as sophisticated as the gilded chest at left.

Ornamentation can be either applied or integral to a piece of furniture. Applied elements are affixed to the basic structure or form; integral elements are built right in. There is beauty in the way that integral ornamentation is inseparable from the structure. Form here is usually the vehicle that provides ornament—a component of the piece is developed to give enriched information, as is the case with the couch in the photo below.

Applying ornamentation is much like decorating a cake or putting on jewelry—adding frills and bits and pieces that are not functionally needed. Applied

ABOVE: The ornamentation in this early 19th-century, Empire-style chest of drawers adds a great deal of sophistication to the piece. The ornament looks applied, as if the piece were dressed in hardware. (Photo courtesy The Metropolitan Museum of Art Rodgers Fund, 1923.)

RIGHT: Ornamentation is integral to the structure and form of this couch by Judy Kensley McKie, of Cambridge, Mass. (Photo by David Caras, collection of Sydney and Frances Lewis.)

FACING PAGE, TOP: This American Art Nouveau sofa attributed to Solomon Isarpen and Brothers (Chicago, 1880-1952), shows how too much ornamentation can lead to gaudiness. (Photo courtesy Museum of Art, Rhode Island School of Design, gift of Mrs. Peter Farago.)

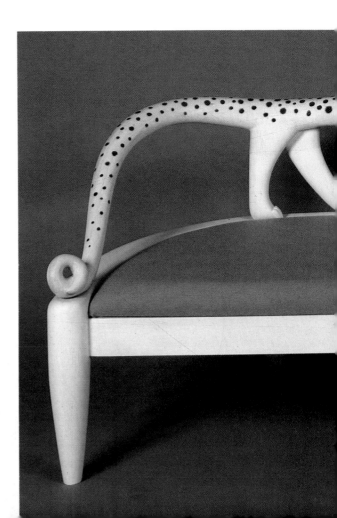

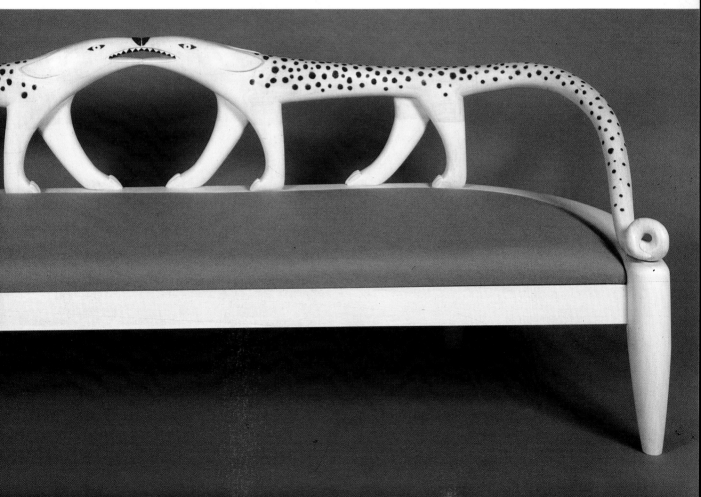

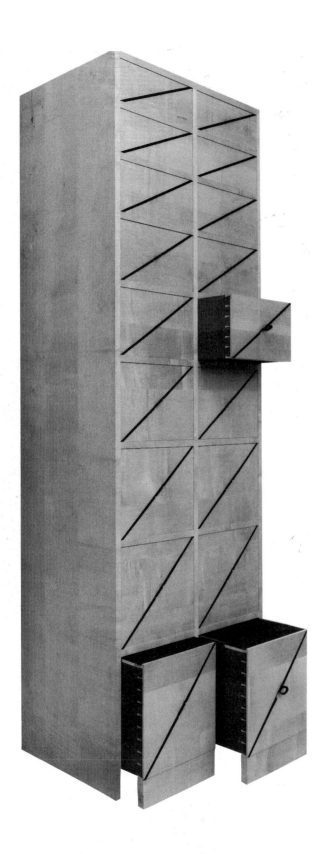

ornamentation can establish a focal point, define an edge or break up a plain surface. It's a way of elaborating or strengthening a design. However, excessive ornamentation can create visual disorder, visual competition among parts or just plain gaudiness, and should be avoided in most cases.

Often, a functional element of a piece can be ornamented with great success—a drawer pull, for instance, could be made highly decorative and larger than necessity dictates. Another approach is to integrate an ornamental pattern into a piece. In the otherwise plain cabinet at left, the unobtrusive ebony inlay creates needed visual interest. As the inlay passes over the face of each drawer, it blends in with a simple ring-shaped ebonite drawer pull. The pull is thus understated, avoiding the interruption that would have been caused had it been positioned to cross the diagonal line, or placed next to it, or made wider than the line itself.

An entire furniture concept may develop from one element that evolves ornamentally. Consider a child's chest of drawers whose goal is to provide a surprise when the drawers are opened. One option

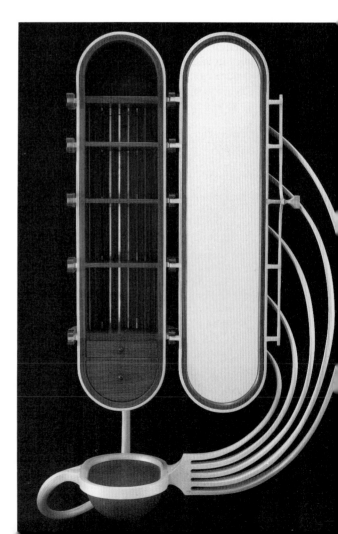

would be tracking the drawer on the sides and concealing the tracking device as a friendly crocodile, which would slide forward when the drawer was opened. Other ideas would be to bandsaw the top edges of the drawer sides in a playful pattern and then paint them, or to add colorful balls along the top edges of the drawers.

The wall-hung cabinet in the photo at right on the facing page also developed ornamentally. The bentwood forms were conceived to provide a resting place for the open cabinet door, so the mirror on the door back would face directly outward. A stop in the door hinges to limit the amount of swing would have performed the same function, but the whole character of the piece would have been different. As it is, the bentwood forms create a sweeping impression when the cabinet is closed, strengthening the composition by balancing the cabinet body and bottom tray.

combining surface treatments

The artful combination of various elements of color, texture and ornamentation can add incredible depth and richness to a piece of furniture. Here are several examples of pieces that I consider to have well-developed surface treatments.

The candle holders of the candlestand in the photo at right are made of patinated copper, and the base is finished with multiple layers of paint and glaze (a varnish medium to which colors can be

FACING PAGE, LEFT: Ebony inlays and ebonite pull rings create a strong diagonal pattern in this otherwise simple cabinet, which was designed by Toby Winteringham and built by Ron Lenthall. The rings are flush with the ebony strips and can be swung out for use. This is a good example of a contemporary piece that directly incorporates function and a decorative element. (Photo by Toby Winteringham.)

FACING PAGE, RIGHT: The bentwood forms of Seth Stem's wall-hung cabinet become a sweeping ornamental element in the composition, as well as providing a resting place for the mirrored door in its open position. (Photo by Mark Harrison.)

RIGHT: The surfaces of this candlestand were developed to simulate metal construction throughout the piece. Furniture designer Rosanne Somerson, of Westport, Mass., and metalsmith Jacqueline Ott, of Providence, R.I., worked together in designing this piece, called Talking House. (Photo by Dean Powell.)

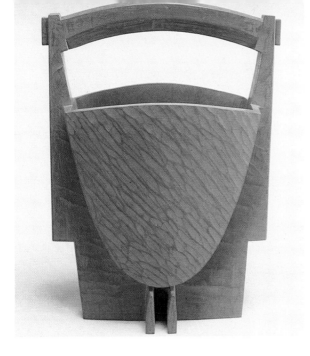

added) over medium-density fiberboard and hardwood. Copper and bronze metallic powders were added to both the paint and the glaze, and the layers were applied with sponges to create the effect of great dimension—it's hard to tell which layer is on the surface and which is under it. The concept of this piece greatly influenced the choice of surface treatment, because the designers wanted the piece to look as though it had a metal core.

A highly developed surface is very likely to become the major feature in a piece. Sometimes designers create objects just because they happen to be interested in surface effects. This approach can have its pitfalls, because there's the risk that the piece will merely look decorated. Surface treatments usually appear more meaningful if they are integrated with other aspects of a piece. As usual, surface treatment is most successful where it supports the concept of the work.

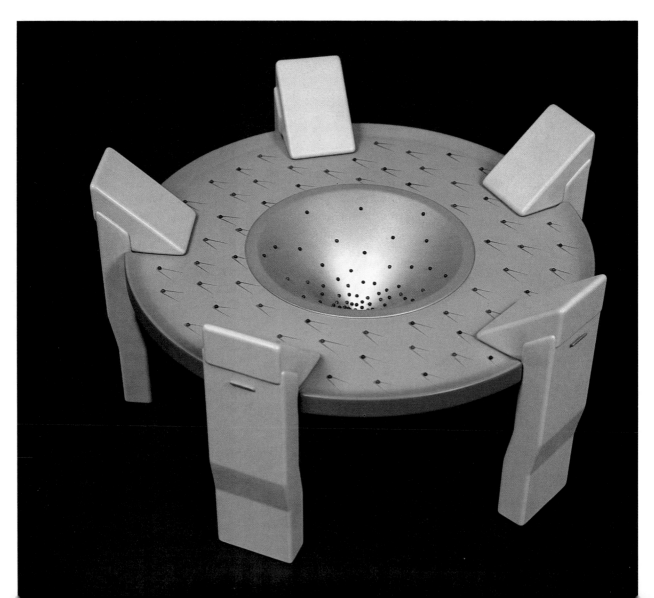

In the vessel in the top photo on the facing page, the form and the surface treatment work as one to suggest agelessness and antiquity. The form is classical; had it been less so, it would not have worked well with the simulated aged surface, which was carved, then painted over and rubbed through with sandpaper. If a piece were designed using this surface technique but with a contemporary or abstract form, the surface treatment might appear superficial and consequently unsuccessful.

The serving tray in the bottom photo on the facing page uses futuristic, structural-looking forms, inlaid plastic beads and painted surfaces to help convey its visual message of extraterrestrial landing crafts and meteorites. On the wide outer ring the beads are uniformly spaced; an airbrushed pattern on the same side of each bead indicates directional airflow. The beads seem to collect in increasing density in the center of the cone-shaped section, as if they were blown inside. This piece has a developed surface because the combination of painting, patterning and texturing all are directed to produce a specific effect.

Layering different colors or types of materials creates interesting surfaces and enhances the feeling of depth. The surface of the cabinet at right was built up by masking and stenciling aniline dyes and Japan oil colors over birch plywood. It is complexly translucent, with one layer blending into another to form patterns and shadings of color. The door patterns are so strong that they dominate the piece. The cabinet was based on fish images—the exterior resembles fish scales, and the interior contains images of small fish.

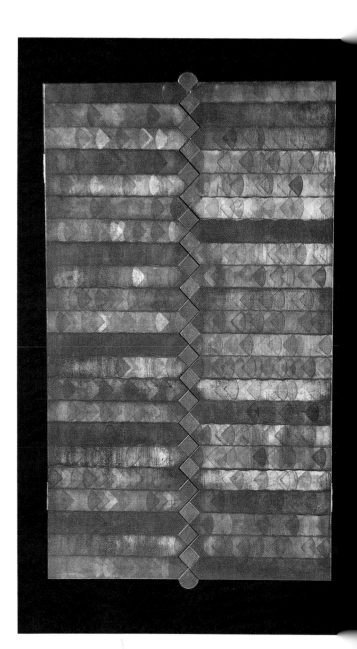

FACING PAGE, TOP: The surface treatment of this carved wooden vessel by Michael Hurwitz, of Philadelphia, Pa., supports the image of antiquity in a classical shape. (Photo by Dean Powell.)

FACING PAGE, BOTTOM: The airbrushed wood surface of this tray by Paul Humaj, of New York, N.Y., was inlaid with small black plastic beads and designed to give an extraterrestrial feeling. (Photo by Seth Stem.)

RIGHT: The doors of this cabinet by Graham Campbell, of Richmond, Va., were stenciled in layers with aniline dyes and Japan oil colors to create a feeling of great depth. (Photo by Graham Campbell.)

DIRECTING THE DESIGN

t's prudent during the design process to step back occasionally and review the status of the design to ensure that your work is evolving along sound aesthetic lines and fulfilling its concept and function. An especially useful group of design tools to aid in this endeavor consists of the elements covered in the first chapter of this section: unity, dominance, repetition and contrast. These elements can and should be considered at many points during design. The issues of character in individual pieces and style within a body of work, discussed in the second chapter in this section, should also be kept in mind, and their development consciously reviewed as the look of the piece begins to take shape. Using these design concepts to inform your judgment at various points in the design process will help you keep sight of the overview as you work, and ultimately strengthen your visual message.

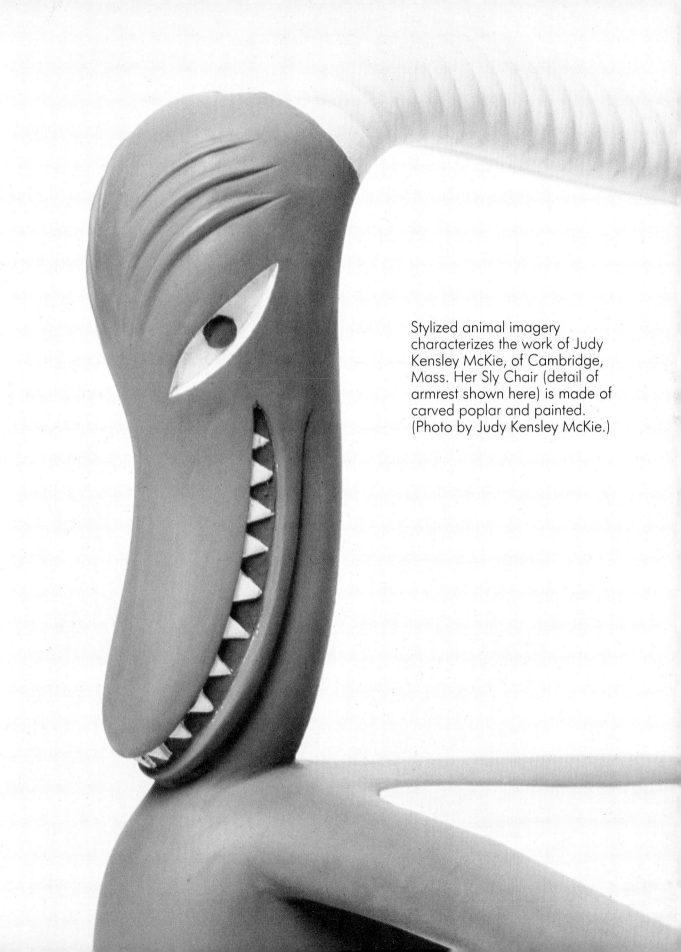

Stylized animal imagery characterizes the work of Judy Kensley McKie, of Cambridge, Mass. Her Sly Chair (detail of armrest shown here) is made of carved poplar and painted. (Photo by Judy Kensley McKie.)

unity, dominance, repetition, contrast

In my own work, while sketching the initial forms of a piece, I'm especially conscious of dominance, repetition and contrast. From that point on, unity becomes paramount as I select materials, detailing and design elements from the visual vocabulary with which to work. But I really never stop evaluating these issues. I ask myself, "Is the repetition of certain lines boring?" "Is more contrast needed?" Most designs have some quality that deserves developing. Perhaps there will be strength in the horizontal lines of a cabinet, which can be manipulated to unify the piece. Or perhaps the horizontal quality could become the dominant visual issue. Through this process of evaluation, the design is continually refined, and sometimes even its entire direction is changed for the better.

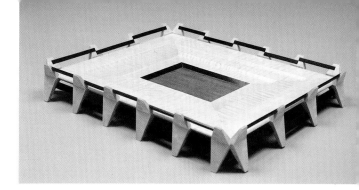

FACING PAGE: In these chairs by Alphonse Mattia of Westport, Mass., the tapered and triangular shapes provide unity and repetition. The triangular section of the back is dominant, because of its dynamic form and position. The use of different colors provides contrast. (Photo by Dean Powell.)

TOP RIGHT: Geometric shapes unify this serving tray by David Page of Philadelphia, Pa. Because of its size and color, the central panel is dominant. The railing is composed of repetitive forms; color, form and changes in visual width add contrast. (Photo by Seth Stem.)

RIGHT: In this padauk, granite and ebony coffee table by Tom Hucker of Charlestown, Mass., the size of the top makes it dominant; the mix of colors and textures adds contrast. The similarity of forms and hierarchy of scale (the base reads as heavy, the stretchers as supports and the details as decoration) create unity. (Photo by Dean Powell.)

BELOW: This couch achieves unity through the upholstery fabric and a simplicity of form. The dominant element is the mass of the cushion grouping. Repetition is created by the three seat cushions and segmented upholstered back; the interplay of rounded armrests and top with the rectangular forms provides contrast. (Photo courtesy of Scandinavian Design/Scandinavian Gallery, Inc.)

When considering unity, dominance, repetition and contrast, beginning designers should be careful not to explore these elements in too obvious a way. Repetition can create unity, but too much of it leads to boring design. In addition, make sure elements do not conflict with each other. If the leg of a chest has a beautiful curve, don't compromise its dominance by adding an adjacent heavy molding around the carcase bottom.

As a last note, keep in mind that as with all other aspects of design (and indeed with the design process itself), it is not always possible to separate one element from another. As you can see in the chair in the photo below left, one characteristic of a piece, such as the stepped armrests, can perform multiple functions, providing repetition and contrast as well as a dominant element.

unity

Essentially, unity works to create a common thread in a design or to tie together various elements. To me, it's synonymous with harmony, and its presence creates oneness, consistency and integration. Without unity, a design will appear disjointed, as if its various elements don't relate. This is not to say, however, that if a piece of furniture looks shocking or discordant, it is necessarily unsuccessful. As strange and contradictory as it may seem, if done well and by design, a powerful lack of unity can be just as effective as a strong sense of unity. (Beginning designers will probably do best, though, to strive for unity.)

In Shaker work, like the cupboard on the facing page, unity is subtle but powerful. The consistent use of square edges and flat planes contributes to the overall effect of unity, as does the monochromatic use of wood. Visual simplicity and straightforwardness enhance the effect, without the eye-catching distractions of ornament, color or overactive form and detail.

Unity is a most difficult quality to pinpoint. This is because it is achieved through associations of elements and not by the presence of a single element. On the other hand, if a piece uses repetition, it's usually fairly obvious. In a wall cabinet whose face is composed of six identical doors, the repetition is clear. If a dining chair has a blue painted foot detail, blue piping around the upholstery and blue slats in the backrest, repetition is blatant.

The unifying element, however, may or may not be related to these characteristics. Unity may be created in the wall cabinet through the composition of the doors, an identical edge detailing on the doors and carcase, or an overall use of veneer. In the chair, the visual width of curved stretchers made of natural wood may relate to the visual width of the straight blue backrest slats. The proportion of the seat may relate to the proportion of the foot detail in an entirely different scale. Unity, therefore, can be achieved by using either common elements or a palette of related elements, such as a group of similar shapes, details, colors or materials. The number of possible relationships is obviously infinite. Following are some examples of pieces that I feel have a strong sense of unity.

The chair above right uses color for unity in several ways. First, orange and blue are complementary colors (see the drawing on p. 111), and thus relate well. Second, the thin line of orange steel outlines the piece and helps tie it together. Third, using different colors to define materials and structural elements also develops a unifying logic.

FACING PAGE, TOP LEFT: This table endlessly repeats the same stepped form. As a result, the piece is predictable and unchallenging to the eye. (Photo by Seth Stem.)

FACING PAGE, BOTTOM LEFT: The stepped armrest of this chair by Hank Gilpin of Lincoln, R.I., is certainly the most dominant element in the piece. The armrest also provides repetition and contrasts with the straight lines of the legs and understructure. (Photo by Seth Stem.)

FACING PAGE, RIGHT: In Shaker work, unity is created primarily through visual simplicity and functional logic. This Connecticut cupboard and case of drawers was made c. 1825-50. (Photo by Paul Rochelean, collection of Mr. and Mrs. Gustave G. Nelson.)

ABOVE: Complementary color unifies this chair by David Dear of Greenwich, Conn. The orange steel framework outlines and ties together the piece. The armrests are made of painted wood. (Photo by Seth Stem.)

BELOW: In this chair by Peter Dean of Charlestown, Mass., the framework creates unity, because it provides consistent color and line weight throughout both the structure and the upholstery. (Photo by Dean Powell.)

FACING PAGE, TOP: Similarity in scale of details is the primary unifying element in this 18th-century American-Dutch lowboy. (Photo courtesy Museum of Art, Rhode Island School of Design, bequest of Charles L. Pendleton.)

FACING PAGE, BOTTOM LEFT: Forms, color, shadowlines and transitional elements unify this lowboy by Peter Spadone of Kennebunk, Maine. (Photo by Dean Powell.)

FACING PAGE, BOTTOM RIGHT: This chair by Terry Cray of Rochester, N.Y., which is an interpretation of the Greek Klismos chair, lacks strong unity. The forms don't work together particularly well, and the contrast between the upholstery and the wood is a bit too strong. (Photo by Matt Matcuk.)

Unity is created in the chair shown in the photo below by the exposed wooden framework, which is of a consistent size, color and visual weight. By running through the back, the framework links the voluminous upholstered areas with the rest of the chair. Also, the negative spaces of the frame relate well to the upholstered segments of the back.

In the contemporary lowboy on the facing page, unity is developed through a variety of artful relationships. The subtle curves in the carcase relate to the curves in the legs. The dividing line between the top and bottom drawers extends onto the sides of the carcase, tying together the front and side views. There is consistency in the way large, plain surfaces relate to details. For instance, the top is punctuated only by the white ball forms, as are the drawer faces by the pulls. The tapered legs are treated at their ends in the same way. Other details that share similar transitional elements are the rings leading into each ball and the fastening plates of the drawer pulls.

Scale and texture are unifying elements in the traditional lowboy on the facing page. The ball-and-claw feet, the carvings at the leg tops, the centered carcase detail and the drawer pulls all relate because of similar size. The texture of the carvings and the pattern of the wood grain also add unity.

The chair in the photo below right lacks a strong sense of unity. The seat and backrest seem applied to the frame, not integrated with it. In addition, the understructure, which uses curves with tapers and flares, does not relate to the frame of the seat and backrest; although curves are present, the frame width is consistent, not variable as in the legs. The color of the upholstery contrasts too harshly with the wood, as does the strong linear pattern with the piece's subtle curves. Also, the orientation of parts seems haphazard (the stretcher is at a different angle from the seat itself, for instance). There are subtle unifying elements present in this piece, such as the use of the same wood throughout and curves of about the same radius, but they are not strong enough to overcome the piece's other shortcomings.

dominance

Every object usually has a dominant element, something that the viewer notices right away. Much of the furniture we live with has a familiar, comfortable appearance that is not meant to be too visually stimulating, but even these familiar pieces have something that will catch the eye. It might be a massive tabletop or the active, beautiful wood grain in a blanket chest. This dominant element focuses the eye and eliminates visual competition.

Dominance may be achieved through a variety of design elements, including color, form, materials and composition. In the drawing on the facing page are some examples of how dominance can work in a piece. In A, dominance is the result of location. The top section of the cabinet dominates the lower section because it is closer to eye level, even though the lower section is larger. (Our eyes have a natural tendency to regard the top part of a composition as more important.) In B, dominance is due to form. This strong wedge shape would dominate most details and materials. Dominance due to color is illustrated at C. At D, the strong diagonal texture of the door panels creates a tremendous amount of visual interest and becomes the focal point.

Naturally, the type and degree of dominance vary from piece to piece, and the issue is frequently more

complex than these drawings suggest. Often the dominant element will be undeniable, but sometimes it may be less evident, perhaps created by combining color, pattern and form. Dominance may even be achieved by a small detail. One color in a piece may be given slightly more value than the others in an analogous color scheme, or a subtle change in line weight may allow the frame of a chair to dominate the stretchers. Each level of dominance can have its own value and place in a design.

In the couch on the facing page, the textures of the upholstery fabric and hardwood frame are subtle

FACING PAGE, TOP: The dominant element in this chair by Josef Hoffmann are the ball details of the back, which create visual interest as well as visual tension through line/form interaction (pp. 74-75) — the balls look as if they are held in place by pressure from the bentwood frame. (Courtesy Museum of Art, Rhode Island School of Design.)

FACING PAGE, BOTTOM: In Reading Couch by Rosanne Somerson of Westport, Mass., the marriage of subtle fabric and bleached, pigmented wenge wood creates an understated but clear dominance. (Photo by Dean Powell.)

CREATING DOMINANT ELEMENTS IN FURNITURE

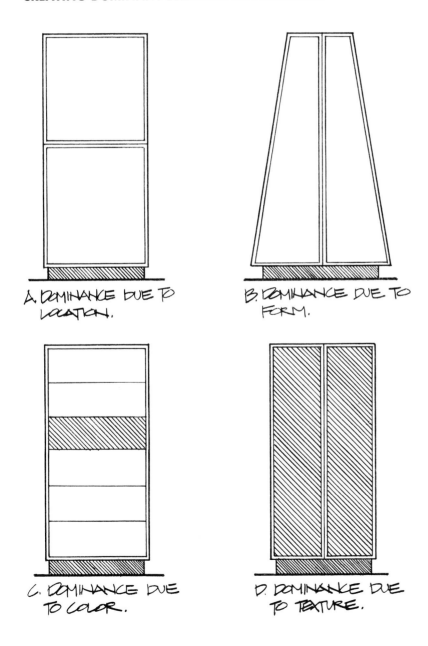

A. DOMINANCE DUE TO LOCATION.

B. DOMINANCE DUE TO FORM.

C. DOMINANCE DUE TO COLOR.

D. DOMINANCE DUE TO TEXTURE.

but dominant features. The wenge wood frame was bleached, then rubbed with a mixture of dried pigment and varnish to accentuate the grain and color. The fabric was carefully chosen to complement the wenge. Together, the textural effects permeate, even create, the piece.

Other features of a piece may be used to play off a dominant element or to strengthen it. For example, although the red used in the spear-shaped back of the bench in the photo below is visually intense, it is overpowered by the directional forms of the entire piece. Here the red calls attention to the dominant directionality of the spear shape, rather than becoming dominant in itself.

repetition

Repetition of a form, detail, material or color can be used to achieve unity in a piece or to add visual power. Repeating an element reinforces its presence. This reinforcement can enhance the development of a visual theme (or a style) or can become the dominant issue in the design. Repetition also lends a visual logic to the work by creating relationships between similar elements.

Repetition is usually always present in a design, sometimes obviously, other times subtly. It does not

The directionality of forms, which is reinforced but not overpowered by the bright red spear, is dominant in this bench by Mark Hazel of Providence, R.I. (Photo by Mark Hazel.)

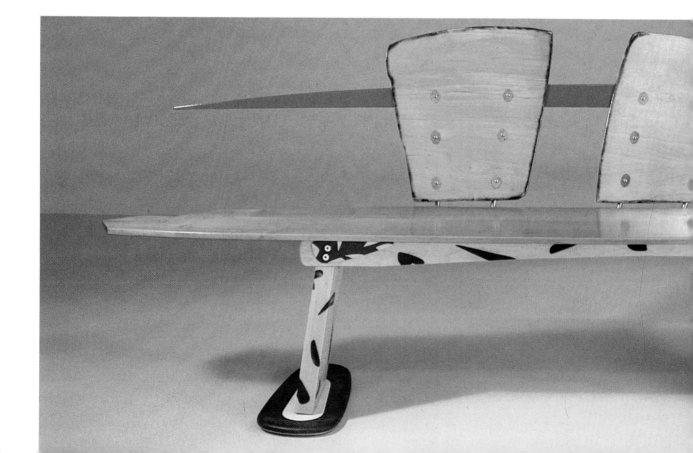

have to be literal to be effective. The cylindrical leg of a desk carried through on a different scale to a drawer pull made of three small connected cylinders is one example of how repetition might work effectively, even though the elements are not directly related in scale or form. Another example is the use of inlaid ¼-in. ebony squares on top of a chair's crest rail relating to a ¼-in. linear dot pattern in the chair's upholstery.

Using repetitive parts to create an overall form can strengthen the visual impact of a piece. A form can also be broken into repetitive parts or details to create more visual interest. Consider the cabinets in the drawing at right. Note that the form of the top cabinet, which is made of connected repetitive carcase sections, has a strong impact; in contrast, the face of the bottom cabinet, which is broken up into repetitive parts through frame-and-panel construction, is interesting, but in a quieter way. Repetition can lead the eye back and forth or in a full three-dimensional journey around an object by causing the eye to follow a certain line weight, color or repeated form.

Stop often to look at your design as it develops. If it seems visually weak or lacks continuity, there may be too many dissimilar forms, details or colors. Introducing a repetitive element might strengthen the design tremendously.

TWO WAYS TO USE REPETITION

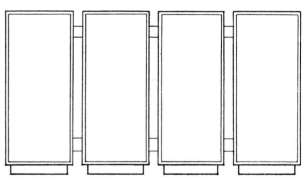

INDIVIDUAL CARCASE SECTIONS CONNECTED TOGETHER MAKE UP THE OVERALL FORM OF THIS CABINET.

HERE A CABINET FACE IS BROKEN UP INTO REPETITIVE FORMS THROUGH THE USE OF FRAME-AND-PANEL CONSTRUCTION.

The table in the photo below is composed of a number of repetitive elements of various forms and sizes. The base has many closely spaced members, which form a massive shelf. The slatted top, which is the primary source of repetition, creates variety through the use of secondary elements—the four areas of negative space and the repetitive cutouts along the front edge. Neither of these secondary elements is entirely regular in spacing. They approximate an arithmetic proportion from right to left. This adds a depth to the design that would have been lacking if pure symmetrical logic had ruled.

Used correctly, repetition reinforces the use of a design element, such as a specific form. It can also help the parts of a piece relate to each other. If the opportunity arises to create a component out of smaller parts used repetitiously, the whole piece may gain more interest. For instance, an upholstered chair seat made up of five cushions may be more appealing than one large cushion; three closely spaced small stretchers in a chair may reinforce a horizontal quality in the piece better than one large stretcher. The color of a tabletop, if carried into the table legs or feet, can visually tie the piece together.

The danger, however, with using repetition is that too much of it can result in an unattractively systematic look. A viewer's interest can quickly fade when one or two elements are used over and over again. This is a problem with the table in the top photo on the facing page. While the idea of using curvilinear forms to carry through the organic quality of the slab tabletop is certainly valid, in this case

BELOW: Repetition is developed in various scales in this table by Tom Hucker of Charlestown, Mass., with the larger forms in the base giving way to delicate slats in the tabletop. Here subtle differences of placement and size create a great deal of interest within similar compositions of parts. (Photo by Dean Powell.)

FACING PAGE, TOP: The curved forms in this table by Paul Ruhlman of Arlington, Mass., bring too much sameness to the work. A contrast in form vocabulary would add visual interest. (Photo by Larry Hunter.)

FACING PAGE, BOTTOM: Carved ivory pieces are used repetitively in Seth Stem's Egyptian Waterway table. Unity is achieved through the use of compositional symmetry, form relationships and color. Scale differences and material variety create strong contrasts. (Photo by Seth Stem, collection of Anne and Ronald Abramson.)

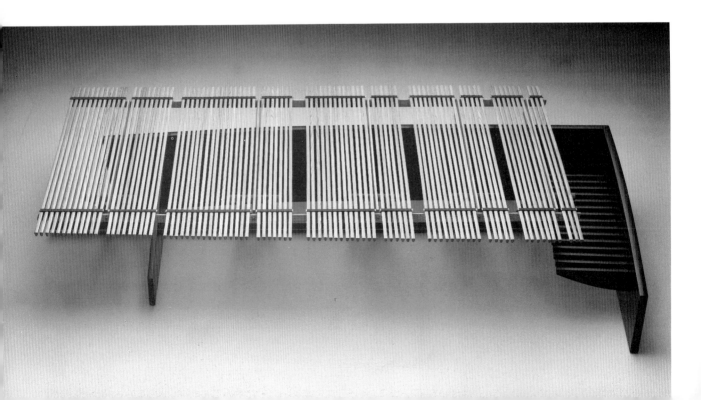

the designer's quest to make things relate resulted in rather too much sameness. The form of the butterfly inlay used to key the check in the slab reflects too closely the form of the table end; the shelf reflects the generally triangular tabletop form; the leg curves reflect all the other curves. Although each element is organic in itself and through repetition supports the intent of the piece, the design would have benefitted from some contrasting forms.

I use a lot of repetition in my work, especially of forms and similar-sized parts. In the table shown below, the repeating elements are the details in the center channel of the top and the four parts of the base. Scale, form and material differences (the details are ivory, the top is ½-in. thick brass and the base is shellacked linen over fiberboard) provide contrast. With this piece I didn't consciously try to create a dominant feature, but felt the top would inevitably become the focal point because of the richness of the ivory and brass. Unity is created through compositional symmetry, form relationships (the channel in the top aligns with the gap between base sections) and by the color match between the ivory and the base. The piece is called Egyptian Waterway because I became intrigued by working with contrasting materials and scales and by using small, wavy, ivory forms repetitively to create an image of water movement. From there I progressed to images of aqueducts, incorporating the buttress-like ends to support a feeling of massiveness. These forms and images related to the idea of Egyptian architecture and waterways, and thus the theme developed.

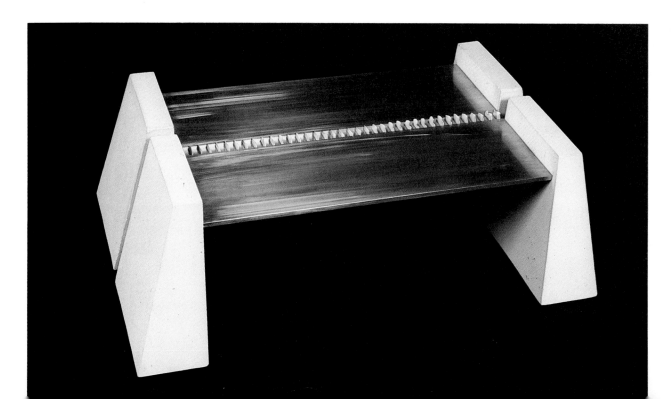

contrast

Contrast keeps a design active, preventing it from becoming visually uneventful and boring. Often the best features of an object are naturally emphasized through contrast—a drawer pull can be an exciting detail in a contrasting material or color and set against a plain drawer front.

All designs have some contrast, because any piece of furniture usually incorporates more than one form, material, detail, line weight, color, pattern or texture. Here again, how a designer manipulates contrast depends on what is suggested by the concept of the design. An aggressive piece of furniture may benefit from a strong use of contrast, while an elegant one might use contrast in a reserved manner. Evaluate the design while it is developing and ask the following questions: Is the use of too much contrast eliminating unity from the design? Could more contrast relieve visual boredom?

Sometimes a furniture designer introduces contrast through an incongruous form or material to give the piece shock value, as in the bench below. Here, contrasting color sets off the flamboyant ends.

Contrast can also be used to create a harmonious relationship. As shown in the drawing on the facing page, a curved line in a form will in some cases read better if it is placed next to a straight line. This is especially true if the curve is subtle, because the straight line then acts as a control against which the curve can be compared. But if the curve is severe,

The incongruous forms of the bench ends provide an interesting contrast in this piece by Garry Knox Bennett of Oakland, Calif. (Photo by Ken Rice.)

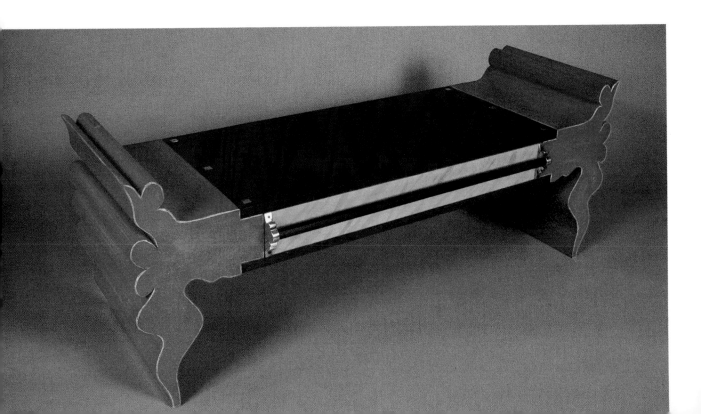

SOME USES OF CONTRAST

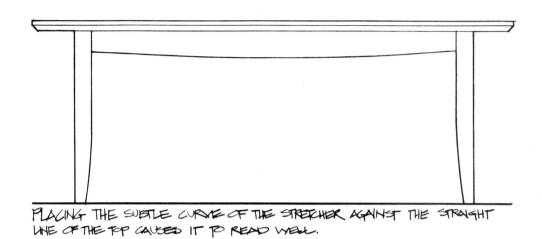

PLACING THE SUBTLE CURVE OF THE STRETCHER AGAINST THE STRAIGHT LINE OF THE TOP CAUSES IT TO READ WELL.

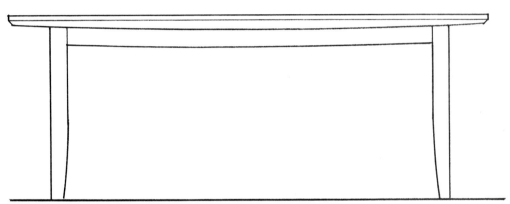

BUT WHEN USED AGAINST A CURVED TOP, THE CURVES BLEND TOGETHER, PLACING LESS OF AN EMPHASIS ON THE STRETCHER FORM.

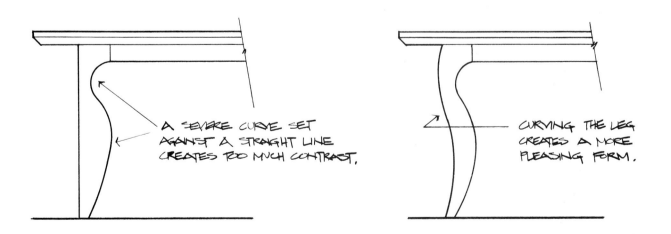

A SEVERE CURVE SET AGAINST A STRAIGHT LINE CREATES TOO MUCH CONTRAST.

CURVING THE LEG CREATES A MORE PLEASING FORM.

The circular seat and back of this chair by Kalle Fauset of New York, N.Y., are emphasized through the use of contrasting colors of the ebonized wood frame and the perforated maple-veneer seat. (Photo by Seth Stem.)

placing it next to a straight line could create a disproportionate contrast and thus discontinuity.

As a general rule, if harmony is sought, a relationship should be constructed between contrasting elements in such a way that the design does not look disorganized or disconcerting. Scale, color, composition, proportion, form and line weight, to name a few elements, can all be used to make visual connections between contrasting elements. For example, in the chair at left, the circular seat and back are emphasized by the black frame, which is in complete contrast to the other colors in the piece. On a cabinet trim detail, different forms could be used around the top and bottom edge—for example, 2-in. triangles at the bottom and 2-in. dia. circles at the top. Although the forms are different, the similar scale would create a relationship. If shock value is the aim, conscious effort should be applied to reduce harmony.

Contrast and dominance are often strong companions and frequently support each other, in that the dominant element usually contrasts with the rest of the piece. In most classic design situations, one of two contrasting elements must fully and clearly dominate the other—one element should act as the backdrop to the other, which is emphasized. A round tabletop made of a colorful wood such as purpleheart, for example, could be contrasted with a black wood base. The base, because of simple form and lack of color, would act as a background to the top, allowing the top to gain dominance. Two elements of equal visual strength create competition and tension, which, unless intentionally desired, can confuse the viewer and detract from the overall effectiveness of the design. The top cabinet in the drawing on the facing page shows how the strong image of an arched door and circle in the center section is challenged by the equally strong diamond-shaped images on the adjacent doors. Essentially this is the wrong kind of contrast, because conflicts are created at the expense of a clear visual message. By comparison, the bottom cabinet keeps the arched center section dominant, contrasting (and complementing) it with decorative circles on the adjacent doors. Because of their small scale and similar form, the circles enhance rather than interfere with the dominant center section.

CONTRAST AND DOMINANCE

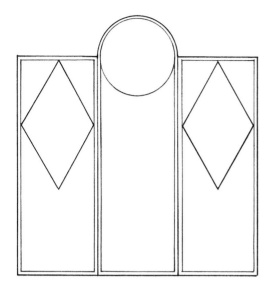

THE STRONG IMAGE OF THE ARCHED DOOR AND CIRCLE IN THE CENTER SECTION OF THIS CABINET IS CHALLENGED BY THE TWO EQUALLY STRONG DIAMOND-SHAPED IMAGES ON THE OUTER DOORS. THIS EXTREME COMPETITION DETRACTS FROM A CLEAR, DOMINANT VISUAL IMAGE.

CONTRAST TO THE RECTILINEAR FORMAT OF THE CABINET IS ACCOMPLISHED THROUGH THE USE OF THE ARCHED CENTER SECTION, WHICH READS AS A DOMINANT FORM. THIS FORM IS COMPLEMENTED BY THE DECORATIVE CIRCLES ON THE OUTER SECTIONS, WHICH, BECAUSE OF THEIR SMALL SCALE AND SIMILAR FORM, DO NOT INTERFERE WITH THE DOMINANT CENTER SECTION.

character and style

character is the feeling evoked in a viewer by a piece of furniture. It can be utilitarian, aggressive, quiet or elegant, to name but a few options. Style refers to a body of work having one or several distinguishable characteristics, usually developed through the use of a consistent palette of design elements. A style can be identified with the work of an individual, a group of people working in a similar vein, a school of thought, a period of time, a nation or a culture. Many types of characters may be developed within a style, as the Art Nouveau pieces shown here illustrate, or the whole concept of a piece may be based on a particular character.

Unlike many of the other elements of design, character and style don't necessarily have to be consciously developed in a furniture project, because they will evolve to some extent just through the normal course of its design and making, as the personality of the designer emerges. The style of Shaker furniture, for example, developed through the makers' concern for function and simplicity. I like to have conscious control over a piece's appearance and how it communicates visually. For example, animated elements may give a piece a humorous character, or a subdued color scheme may create a serene feeling. If the concept of a piece concerns massiveness, you could develop a clean, contemporary piece with large flat surfaces and plain, heavy structural members (such as the dresser on p. 76) or a Gothic-style piece heavily embellished with carvings. The char-

LEFT: This Art Nouveau chair made by Charles Rohlfs of Buffalo, N.Y., has limited decoration, which contrasts with the larger unadorned areas and results in a utilitarian character. (Photo courtesy Boston Museum of Fine Art, gift of a friend of the department and the Arthur Mason Knapp Fund.)

FACING PAGE: Organic carvings, attention to detail in the base and decorative upholstery give an ornate character to this Art Nouveau oak side chair, also by Rohlfs. (Photo courtesy Art Museum of Princeton University, gift of Roland Rohlfs.)

acter and style you select make a world of difference in the viewer's perception of the piece and in the visual message the piece expresses.

I find it useful periodically to step back from the work and evaluate the character and style that might be developing. At the very least, I review the character and style of a piece during the sketching stage of design. Then I check my intent while doing working drawings to ensure that form and detail retained their original thrust during design development.

character

The character developed in a furniture piece may be influenced by its materials, structure or function, or by any visual references or icons that are selected. If a piece is made from industrial materials and shapes, for instance, it will probably have a technical look. If the work is referenced to animal imagery, there is every chance it will look animated. Character may also be established by the concept, as in a line of children's furniture based on a cartoon series.

Naturally, developing character in a piece is much more than a matter of manipulating form, composition, color, texture and other elements of the visual vocabulary. As in all of design, creating a successful piece requires vision and imagination. Because developing character and style demands a synthesis of design elements and ideas, there are no guidelines—every designer will take a unique approach. You'll

BELOW: The form of an isolated facial feature is the basis for this bizarre couch, designed by Studio 65 for Stendig, Inc., New York, N.Y. Marilyn Monroe's lips are made of stretch fabric over foam. (Photo by Seth Stem.)

FACING PAGE: Pedro Friedeberg of Mexico City, Mexico, gave his clock a whimsical character by substituting hands and fingers for the numbers usually used on the face. (Photo courtesy Phyllis Needlman Gallery, Chicago, Ill.)

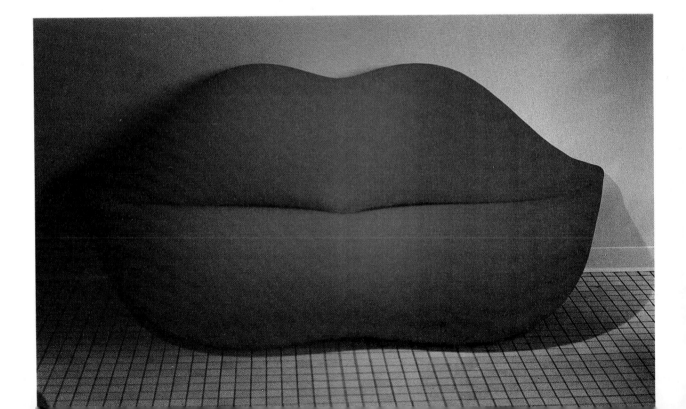

learn best by visual study. Following are some examples of ways in which furniture designers have
manipulated design elements to portray character in
their work; a look at many of the other photos in
this book will provide additional food for thought.

The human hands in the clock shown below give
this piece its whimsical character. The animated
form of the legs supports the essence of the hands;
in addition, because the linear legs point to the center of the clock body as they enter the circular form,
they add visual logic to the design. (See the discussion on line/form interaction, pp. 74-75.) The natural state of the wood also complements the clock's
character, relating as it does to the feeling of skin.

In the loveseat on the facing page, form and color
translate the sensuous image of Marilyn Monroe's
bright red lips into a seating function. Extraneous
elements were eliminated in this piece so the image
of the lips would read clearly. Structure is disguised,
and the piece is devoid of the usual details of fabric
seams and base element. This piece, which is a modern interpretation of surrealist Salvador Dali's couch

design, has a bizarre character, which becomes especially evident when someone is viewed sitting on it. (Dali often took various objects and put them in an environment that was abnormal or bizarre.)

The character of the dressing table and chair on the facing page can only be described as ornate. These pieces are an example of how a design element (ornamentalism) can dictate the character of a piece. The desk is heavily inlaid on all surfaces with floral patterns of silver, ivory and mother-of-pearl and embellished with applied silverwork on the legs, feet, mirror support and mirror. Other elements of design also are used to complement the piece's character. The rich black background contrasts with the ivory and silver patterns. Variations in line weight range from the heavy legs to the medium weight of the tabletop edge to the fine lines of the inlay. The variations and combinations of these line weights create a variety of patterns and forms that support the ornate character of the piece. Repetition (the silver banding details around the desk edge and chair seat are an example) adds order and logic, as does the composition of the aligning panels (these help strengthen the organic ornamental quality by providing a geometric counterpoint). The cabriole legs support the organic patterns of the inlay.

The chairs shown below, which are typical of the style of the designer, have a flamboyant character

FACING PAGE: The Gorham Silver Co. of Rhode Island was well known for its intricate designs using precious materials. William Codman designed this dressing table and chair for Gorham in 1903 of silver, ivory, mother-of-pearl and black lacquer over wood. Its character can only be described as ornate. (Photo courtesy Museum of Art, Rhode Island School of Design, gift of Mr. and Mrs. Frederick B. Thurber.)

BELOW: A flamboyant character was developed in this chair series by Jay Stanger of Charlestown, Mass., through the use of bright colors, lively and incongruous forms, asymmetry and directionality as the main elements of the visual vocabulary. (Photo by Dean Powell.)

THIS PAGE: Humorous references in this valet series by Alphonse Mattia of Westport, Mass., include Potato Head (fourth from left), Brains (sixth from left) and Knot Head (seventh from left). (Photo by Dean Powell.)

FACING PAGE, TOP: The foam-rubber tentacles of Sea Anemone Chair by Larry Hunter of Long Beach, Calif., envelop the sitter. (Photo by Larry Hunter.)

FACING PAGE, BOTTOM: This chair by Eliel Saarinen has an elegant character due to its crisp forms, attention to detail and sophisticated back. (Photo collection of Cranbrook Academy of Art Museum.)

that arises from the use of form, composition and color. Many of the forms are arched and wedge-shaped, and their composition plays a straight side off a curved side. Flamboyance also comes from the looseness and freedom of the design, and from the allusion to visual chaos. In reality, however, chaos is offset by strict visual order. Repetition of curved forms is used in the chair to the left, color separates lines and planes in the center chair, and a strong directional quality is established by the back and seat of the chair at right.

The valet series on the facing page has a humorous character, which pokes fun at both common idioms and woodworking techniques. The pieces in the series almost always elicit a chuckle from first-time observers. The carved kinks and twists in all the structures and the painted waterfall wood-grain veneer on Potato Head's seat (fourth from left) are comments on how woodworkers often try to push their materials to the technical limit. In these pieces, the ornamentation is integrated, in that the normal parts of a valet, such as the seat and backrest, were manipulated and developed to create a humorous image. The posture of the chairs and their high backs suggest tall, skinny people patiently standing with outstretched arms, waiting to be dressed. The character of the work develops largely from vertically extended proportion and posture, both of which help lighten the tone of the valets. Color is used unobtrusively, so it doesn't detract from the forms, but separates some of the parts of the chairs. This serves to focus attention on seats and backrests, because these are the elements that introduce humorous information. Other visual information is carefully handled so it does not compete with the message of humor. Structure is kept to a minimum so the visual message is uninterrupted; there are no more stretchers between legs or in the backrests than are absolutely necessary to support the minimal function of the pieces.

When the sea anemone at top right is used, the sitter experiences the lifelike character of the chair firsthand. It's made of paper-mâché and stretch fabric over foam rubber. When a person sits on it, the center pad lifts the bright red tentacles up around its captive; the rounded bottom tilts and rocks. The recognizable natural imagery was transferred directly to the piece, but edited and embellished by the designer. For instance, the tentacles do not have the same proportion, form or detail as on the sea anemone, but were portrayed in stylized form. The piece is also altered dramatically in color to add to the fun and provide a dominant element.

The chair at bottom right derives its elegant character from classical form, proportion, posture, symmetrical composition, precise detailing, variety of

line weights, rich materials and color. The tapering thickness of the back relates to the taper of the dark inlays on both surfaces. The forms are crisp and refined, and the linear quality of the piece is enhanced both by the linear fabric pattern and by the use of various line weights of the same dark color throughout the chair. In this chair, the absence of elements and the reduction of visual information are just as important in creating character as the elements that are in evidence.

In contrast, consider the chair at left. Here bone-like images and color combine with stained leather in a tiger-skin pattern to create a primitive character. Asymmetry in composition adds to the feeling of primitivism, because the organic forms we see in nature are primarily asymmetrical or viewed in a natural, asymmetrical setting. The lack of detailing and

LEFT: A primitive character was developed in this chair, one of a series by Keith Crowder of Providence, R.I., through the use of bone-like images and color and a bold tiger-skin pattern on the seat. (Photo by Seth Stem.)

BELOW: Robert Wilson of Glen Cove, N.Y., gave this bench a high-tech character because he wanted to support the structural concept relating to bicycle-wheel suspension. (Photo by Robert Wilson.)

FACING PAGE: This table by Marissa Brown of Alexandria, Va., has clean lines and a visual spareness. Although quite functional and lovely in its simplicity, it doesn't have a memorable character. (Photo by Seth Stem.)

edging in the upholstery also lends itself to the direct, unsophisticated construction methods that are associated with primitivism.

The bench on the facing page has a high-tech character which comes from the forms and materials in the tension/compression system of suspending the seat from the leg sections. The sandblasted steel surface of the structure and the black leather upholstery help to support the bar, cylinder and rod form vocabulary that was used. The concept of this piece came from looking at spoked bicycle wheels and transferring not only the method by which a hub is seemingly held in suspension in the center of a wheel, but also the character of a slick, high-technology look that state-of-the-art bicycles take on.

The more forcefully design elements are used, the more likely will be the development of a strong character. The opposite is also true. The table at right, for instance, is a piece that would be easy to live with. It is nicely proportioned and has a pleasing form, but lacks the strong level of visual information that would give it a palpable character. Adding more parts, such as a series of horizontal stretchers, or using other design elements like color or texture might start to develop a character, but there are also other solutions. Animating the form of the legs, for example, would immediately make the piece more distinct without increasing its complexity.

style

With experience, any designer can create a style and apply it across an entire body of work. It is a matter of formulating a design philosophy and gathering together a personal palette of design elements within which to work. Some furniture designers evolve a recognizable furniture style over the years by working within a relatively circumscribed visual vocabulary. Others endlessly attempt new styles or continually create variations of existing styles.

Generally, designers tend to hold on to at least some of the details, colors or forms that have proved successful in past work and explore new boundaries of this palette with each new design. As new inspirations occur, new elements are added to the palette, and gradually a recognizable style evolves. The furniture of Judy Kensley McKie, a well-known furniture maker (see the photos of her furniture on pp. 120-121 and p. 127), has a recognizable style that is connected to the use of a particular design palette of Egyptian-like carved animal imagery, subtle color and playfulness.

As with the issue of character in furniture, visual analysis is the best way to understand how designers

use various elements to create a style. A good starting point is furniture of the past. Volumes have been written about historical styles of furniture, significant designers and materials and processes; consult your local library for some leads. Here let's consider a few examples of pieces created from a variety of historical movements and personal palettes.

The style that evolved in the postwar furniture of California architect Charles Eames amalgamated a concern for technology and a perception of a common need of comfort with his own aesthetic point of view. Forms such as the compound-curved plywood chair and the molded fiberglass chair shown in the photos at left were specifically developed to take advantage of new manufacturing processes. I don't consider many of these mass-produced pieces particularly appealing to look at, but their style is a reflection of Eames' innovative thinking in the Modernist style.

Quite a different style is apparent in the furniture of architects Charles and Henry Greene, brothers whose work expresses the aesthetic of the Arts and Crafts movement in the United States. Typical of their furniture is the 1907 armchair shown on the facing page. The chair is made of finely finished hardwood and uses accentuated joinery and softened edges. Additional recurring elements are a subtle stepped motif in the framework, which lends a slight Chinese character, and raised-peg details in contrasting wood.

A style may also develop out of a process, as in the work of Michael Thonet, a 19th-century German cabinetmaker. Thonet's bentwood style evolved from a breakthrough in steam-bending. The development of a method of producing curves with tight radii through the use of a backing strap permitted the use of tangentially connected curves and loops in furniture. An example of the bentwood style is shown in the top photo on p. 157.

THIS PAGE: The style of these chairs by Charles Eames evolved from explorations of new materials, manufacturing processes and comfort in seating. (Top photo courtesy Museum of Art, Rhode Island School of Design, Providence, R.I.; bottom photo courtesy Museum of Modern Art, New York, N.Y., gift of Herman Miller Furniture Company.)

FACING PAGE: This Blacker House chair by Charles and Henry Greene is given a slight Chinese character by the recurring use of a stepped motif. (Photo courtesy Los Angeles County Museum of Art, promised gift of Jodie Evans and Max Palevsky.)

The style of the chairs shown below (part of a series of five) was based on saddle imagery. Wood was the primary material, and saddle forms with pommels became dominant visual elements. Bentwood structures added an active, animated posture. Function was not a primary issue; the designer was more concerned with what the pieces conveyed visually and how an association might be made to the different ways we can sit—on a fence, in the crotch of a tree and, most important to the designer, in a saddle. Minimal support to the user's body was also an important issue in this series.

The pieces in the bottom photo on the facing page (part of a series) were designed for a major contract-furniture company by Wendell Castle. The vocabulary used included painted cone-shaped legs with small brass balls at the top and doughnut-shaped feet. The style was outrageous for office furniture, and few of the pieces sold. However, the series drew a lot of attention to the Gunlocke furniture showroom, which was the intent of the marketing department, so the furniture was highly successful on that level.

developing an individual style   To develop a new style, or simply to understand style better, try this exercise. Select a specific palette of design elements, and then develop two or three pieces of furniture working from this selection. You might, for

BELOW: William Hammersley of Richmond, Va., developed a personal style through this chair series by using abstractions of saddle images coupled with bentwood forms. (Photos by William Hammersley; photo below left, collection of Museum of Art, Rhode Island School of Design, Providence, R.I.)

FACING PAGE, TOP: This bentwood chair is a more recent version of the original Vienna Chair designed by Michael Thonet (1796-1871), who was perhaps the most successful furniture maker in history. The style of his furniture evolved through the development of the bentwood process, through which beautiful curvilinear forms could be realized. (Photo by Seth Stem.)

FACING PAGE, BOTTOM: A strong form vocabulary of cone-shaped legs and doughnut-shaped feet was used by Wendell Castle of Scottsville, N.Y., to create the Atlantis table, desk and chair—a radically new style of contract furniture for the Utopia collection of the Gunlocke Co. (Photo by Myers Studio, Orchard Park, N.Y.)

example, choose the following: symmetry in composition; strong geometric forms such as triangles, circles and rectangles; strong color or value contrast between details and the rest of the piece; and the use of small-scale, delicate detailing as a transition or point of accent wherever a structural element becomes larger or smaller. (Here again, a visual reference or icon, as discussed on pp. 34-40, may be extremely useful as a start in developing the visual vocabulary.) Some of these elements may be consciously chosen before sketching begins, others may be added as sketching progresses. Remember, sketching is only the beginning of the design process, and for most of us it provides only a glimpse of an idea. Have confidence that the ideas you sketch are good, and just need to be run through the design process. This will keep you from flitting from sketch to sketch of different ideas in search of the "perfect" one.

In the sketch series on pp. 158-159, the design elements are symmetry; a central detail; 45° angles and triangles; tall, slender feet; and small circle details. The visual reference is high-heeled shoes, which affects the posture of the piece as well as the leg and foot forms. Some of the elements were dropped in certain pieces, such as the triangles in the chest at bottom left on p. 158, and different elements added, such as the dentil detailing in the same chest. Note that although the piece at bottom right on p. 159 incorporates much of the same vocabulary as the

AN EXERCISE IN STYLE DEVELOPMENT

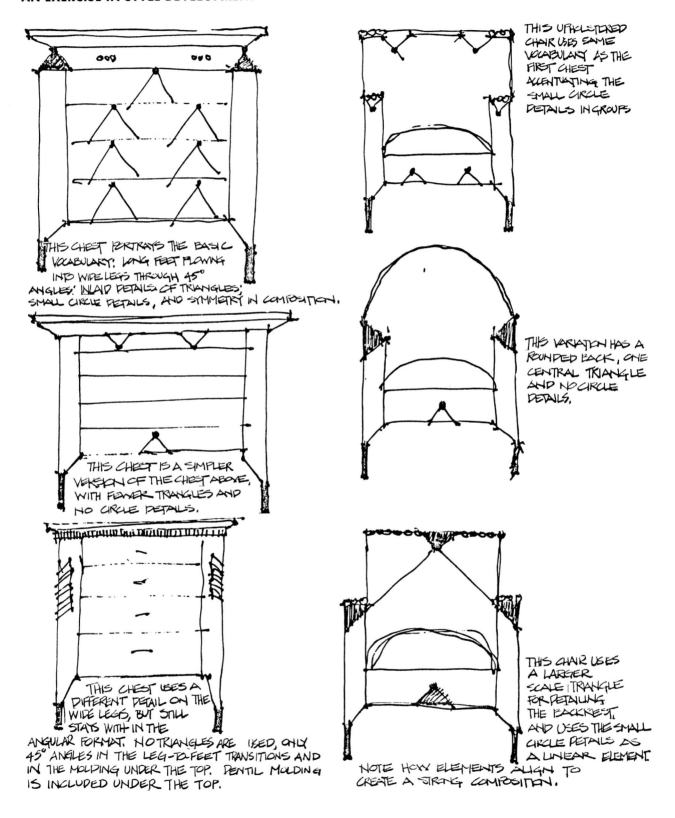

THIS CHEST PORTRAYS THE BASIC VOCABULARY: LONG FEET FLOWING INTO WIDE LEGS THROUGH 45° ANGLES; INLAID DETAILS OF TRIANGLES, SMALL CIRCLE PETALS, AND SYMMETRY IN COMPOSITION.

THIS CHEST IS A SIMPLER VERSION OF THE CHEST ABOVE, WITH FEWER TRIANGLES AND NO CIRCLE DETAILS.

THIS CHEST USES A DIFFERENT DETAIL ON THE WIDE LEGS, BUT STILL STAYS WITH IN THE ANGULAR FORMAT. NO TRIANGLES ARE USED, ONLY 45° ANGLES IN THE LEG-TO-FEET TRANSITIONS AND IN THE MOLDING UNDER THE TOP. DENTIL MOLDING IS INCLUDED UNDER THE TOP.

THIS UPHOLSTERED CHAIR USES SAME VOCABULARY AS THE FIRST CHEST, ACCENTUATING THE SMALL CIRCLE DETAILS IN GROUPS

THIS VARIATION HAS A ROUNDED BACK, ONE CENTRAL TRIANGLE AND NO CIRCLE DETAILS.

THIS CHAIR USES A LARGER SCALE TRIANGLE FOR DETAILING THE BACKREST, AND USES THE SMALL CIRCLE PETALS AS A LINEAR ELEMENT. NOTE HOW ELEMENTS ALIGN TO CREATE A STRONG COMPOSITION.

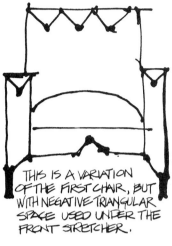

THIS IS A VARIATION OF THE FIRST CHAIR, BUT WITH NEGATIVE TRIANGULAR SPACE USED UNDER THE FRONT STRETCHER.

THIS TABLE USES THE BASIC PALETTE OF ELEMENTS.

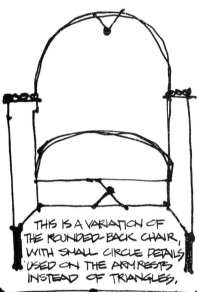

THIS IS A VARIATION OF THE ROUNDED-BACK CHAIR, WITH SMALL CIRCLE DETAILS USED ON THE ARM RESTS INSTEAD OF TRIANGLES.

THIS VARIATION ELEVATES THE TOP ABOVE THE STRETCHERS TO PROVIDE A STRONG NEGATIVE SPACE. THE TRIANGULAR DETAIL SLIPPED BELOW THE STRETCHER LINE BECOMES AN INTERESTING FORM IN ITSELF.

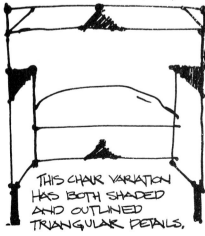

THIS CHAIR VARIATION HAS BOTH SHADED AND OUTLINED TRIANGULAR DETAILS.

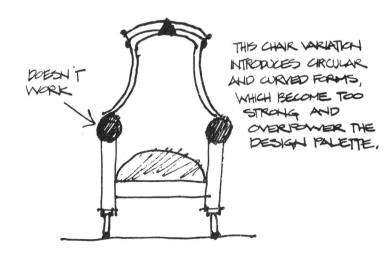

DOESN'T WORK

THIS CHAIR VARIATION INTRODUCES CIRCULAR AND CURVED FORMS, WHICH BECOME TOO STRONG AND OVERPOWER THE DESIGN PALETTE.

other pieces in the series, it doesn't work because the curvilinear forms contrast too strongly with the geometric feel of the other pieces.

Included in the palette of design elements are usually forms or details that create a common thread from piece to piece. As you work, try to transfer the essence of a design from one piece to another. This doesn't mean that if one piece has four distinct elements, all the rest must have the same four elements, for this would be both extremely difficult and probably a bit boring. There should be a common thread, but best results come from similarities, not a sameness. (If each piece has exactly the same identity, then a collection of furniture is developed, such as a matching bedroom set.) Allow yourself the latitude of creativity—in changing the scale of a detail, altering a form, adding a new element. It is this interplay from piece to piece that not only creates variety and interest in a style, but also expands its possibilities or increases its sophistication.

As the number of explorations increases, individual style becomes much more apparent. As variations occur, refinements are made and a collective statement develops. Korean style, for instance, is the result of centuries of tradition; an example is shown in the photo on the facing page. Mission furniture represents a school of thought within the Arts and Crafts movement in the early 1900s. Sam Maloof's furniture (see the rocking chair on p. 46) represents the work of one man over many years using about the same visual and technical vocabulary in his work.

In developing a style, we are naturally influenced by the images we see around us every day of trends in furniture, fashion and advertising. If we use these influences, we probably will design a piece that fits into the existing style of the times. If a new style is intended, carefully creating and editing the visual vocabulary can help. The style may not gain any sort of general approval, for people are typically resistant to change—witness the automobile industry, where essentially the same style is re-issued year after year. It's a lot easier to fit into an existing style than to create a new one. More than likely any new design work you may develop would become a new twist on an existing style rather than a whole new style, which is fine. Within any given style, there is lots of room for personal statements and new contributions.

FACING PAGE: Style can be influenced by history or by a culture, as was this acacia-patterned small clothing chest by Sung-Soo Kim of Seoul, Korea. His work is within the Korean tradition practiced over many centuries. (Photo by Han Seok-Hong Photo Studio.)

THEORY INTO PRACTICE: APPENDICES

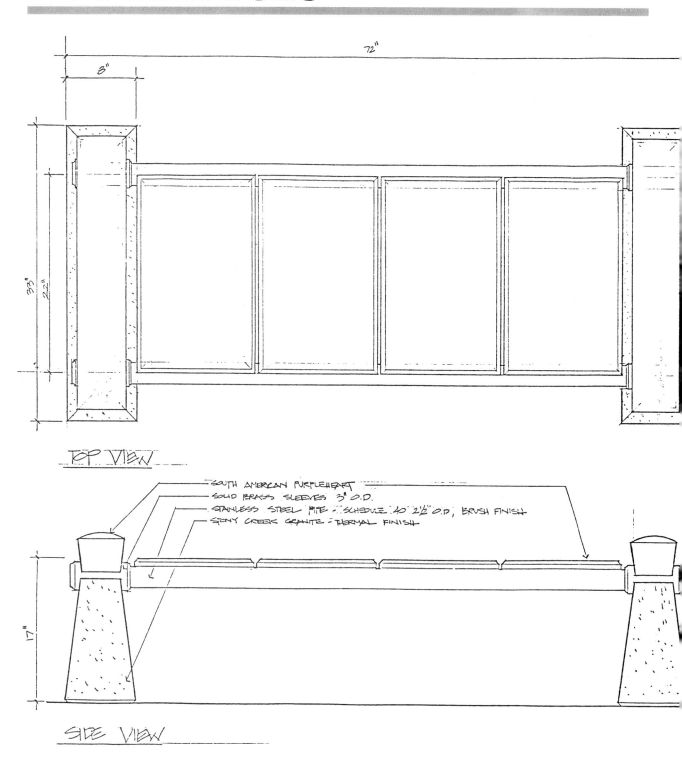

72"

8"

33"

2.2"

TOP VIEW

SOUTH AMERICAN PURPLEHEART
SOLID BRASS SLEEVES 3" O.D.
STAINLESS STEEL PIPE - SCHEDULE 40 2½" O.D, BRUSH FINISH
STONY CREEK GRANITE - THERMAL FINISH

17"

SIDE VIEW

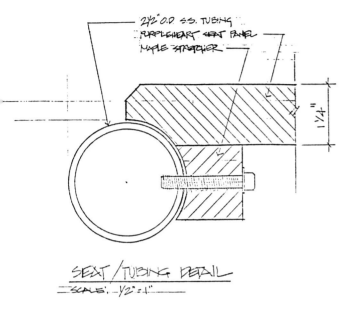

2½" O.D. S.S. TUBING
PURPLEHEART SEAT PANEL
MAPLE STRETCHER

1¼"

SEAT/TUBING DETAIL
SCALE: ½" = 1"

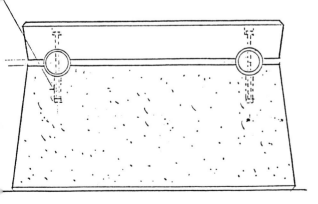

½ DIA. BOLT - GROUT INTO GRANITE BASE

END VIEW

BRIDGEPORT CRIMINAL COURTHOUSE
STATE OF CONNECTICUT
COMMISSION ON THE ARTS

BENCH PROPOSAL
SETH L STEM, ARTIST
JULY 1988

A. tools for creating working drawings

Working drawings show how a project will be built, and also how the proportions and details of each element will come together visually. They can be orthographic projections (top, front and end views of an object), isometrics (a three-dimensional view in which true dimensions are shown on three axes) or perspectives (a view of the object as it would appear to the eye from a given viewing point); see pp. 168-185 for details. Sometimes I use a combination of all three drawing types.

It's a good idea to make working drawings at the point when the design is beginning to take final form—what I call the "design development" stage (see pp. 18-34). Working drawings usually carry final dimensions, but these are often modified as the design is refined. To do working drawings you'll need an architect's scale, a drafting table, a T-square or parallel rule with triangles or a drafting machine, pencils and drafting paper.

architect's scale I try to draw furniture (or at least certain parts) to full scale whenever possible. The advantage is that I can see exactly how big a piece will be and the size of all its components. It's usually easy to get overall dimensions correct at any scale, but the details and dimensions of individual parts are sometimes difficult to visualize at anything less than full scale. Full-scale drawings can also be used as patterns or templates. You simply trace around the drawing or glue it directly to the construction material with spray adhesive and cut around it.

One disadvantage of full-scale drawings is that they can be cumbersome, and the size of your drafting table limits the size of the piece—I can't fit any-

thing much bigger than a chair or a small table on mine. At times I've pieced together drawings so I can create larger pieces, but this can be inconvenient. Furniture makers who have the space might make a drawing board out of a 4x8 sheet of plywood to keep in the shop, and leave the drawings on the board to refer to during construction.

When full-scale drawings aren't possible, I work with an architect's scale, which is a rule having measurements representing up to 11 different scales. It's easy to read an architect's scale, but if you don't know how, ask the salesperson where you buy yours for a quick demonstration. I usually work so that a fraction of an inch equals an inch, for example, so that ¼ in. equals 1 in. The proportion could also be represented as ¼ ft. equals 1 ft. or any other convenient measurement. Many times I will draw the top, front and end views of a piece in one scale and the details in a larger scale. I try not to mix scales in the three basic views, however, because even a momentary lapse in attention can cause an expensive mistake in the shop. Using a ¼-in. scale to pick dimensions off a part of a drawing done in ⅛-in. scale, for instance, will lead to the production of parts twice the intended size. It is best to dimension all parts of your drawing so a scale does not have to be used in the shop.

drafting tables and accessories To create accurate working drawings, you must use a good drafting table. Mine is 34 in. wide by 48 in. long, which is adequate for most scaled drawings but a bit small for full-size work. (A 4x6 or 4x8 surface is optimum for full-scale drawings.) The table should be fitted with a T-square or a parallel rule for constructing horizontal lines, or a drafting machine, which also draws vertical and angled lines. The drafting machine (see the photo on the facing page) is fastest and easiest to use, but is also more expensive; the T-square is least expensive, but you constantly have to hold it against the edge of the table. If you use a T-square, make sure the edge it rides on is straight (a hardwood edge cap is a good idea). A straight edge isn't necessary when using a drafting machine or parallel rule.

A drafting machine consists of an adjustable arm or track system that holds two graduated scales at right angles in a rotating mechanism. The scales can be maneuvered to any position on the drawing and rotated to form any angle. (Photo by Seth Stem, equipment courtesy Charrette Corp.)

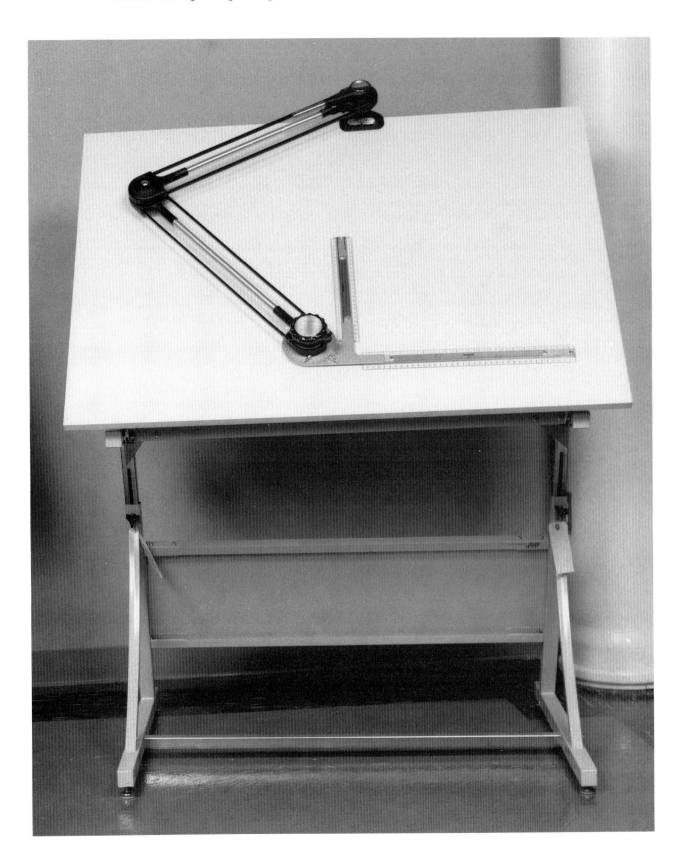

With a T-square or parallel rule, use triangles to draw vertical and angled lines. Drafting triangles all have one 90° angle. Some triangles have 45° angles, and some have 30° and 60° angles; other triangles are adjustable to any angle. Don't buy a cheap triangle because the edges will roughen with use or even chip. Draw circles with a circle template, a drafting compass or beam compass for large arcs. Use a French curve or flexible curve to draw spirals and organic shapes.

pencils and leads I organize line weights in my working drawings to separate the lines of the piece from other information, such as dimension lines or leaders. The drawing on the facing page shows different line weights and how I use them. I draw with a mechanical pencil rather than a wooden one because the lead quality is consistently excellent. Lead is classified according to hardness, as follows:

B *Very soft.* Ranges from 7B, the softest, to B.
HB *Soft.*
F *Slightly harder than HB.*
H *Hard.* Ranges from H, the softest, to 9H, which is extremely hard.

B and HB leads make very dark lines because the soft lead easily transfers to the paper, but they also break and blunt easily. I use them only for shading and sketching, not for drafting. Most of the time I use 2H lead for everything, because the point holds up well and the line is nice and dark. Sometimes I'll use H for the dark lines of a drawing, 2H for most of the other lines and 4H for fine lines and dimensioning. For very fine, light lines you can use 7H and 9H leads, but it's easy to tear the paper with these.

Line weights are not a function of how dense a line is, but rather of how wide it is. Construction lines, which I make faint as well as very narrow, are the exception to this. I apply very little pressure with the lead when drawing these lines because I don't want them noticeable in the final drawing. To make a thin line, I'll usually make one pass with my pencil and 2H lead, applying a reasonable amount of pressure (too much and the point will break), and

slowly spinning the pencil between my fingers so the lead doesn't flatten out on one side. To make a wider line, I'll draw two or more sharp, thin lines side by side so they blend together into one. If you make a wide line with a dull lead, the edges of the line will be fuzzy and, if the line is long, its width will vary.

drafting paper I use drafting vellum for most of my working drawings. This is a high rag-content paper that's translucent, so prints can be made from it. Prints can't be made from ordinary paper, and more than once I wished I had used vellum on a project so I could make a copy of the drawings before cutting them up for templates. Vellum comes in different weights, the heavier ones standing up better to wear and tear and erasures. I generally use 17-lb. paper. Vellum comes in various sizes in both rolls and precut sheets. I prefer precut sheets, because then I don't have to worry about cutting straight edges from a roll or the paper curling up on the drafting board. Vellum has a "tooth" to one or both surfaces, which allows it to pick up pencil lead well and to be erased easily. Buy double-toothed vellum so you can draw on both sides or shade the back if need be. Mylar, a plastic drafting film, is more durable and more forgiving of erasure, but it costs about three times as much as vellum.

blueprints Prints can be made from drafting vellum or Mylar at any blueprint company. Actually, blueprinting has long been superseded by the diazo process, in which blackline or blueline prints are made on a whitish background (blueprints have white lines on a dark-blue background). I almost always work from diazo prints in my shop so the originals won't get dirty, wrinkled or lost—I also put notes and changes on the prints. However, if I am going to use full-scale drawings of furniture parts as patterns or templates and these have to be absolutely accurate, I generally use the original drawings instead. During the printing process it's not unusual for a print to be stretched ¼ in. longer than the original drawing.

LINE WEIGHTS

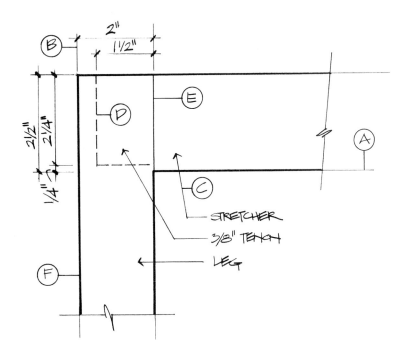

A. CONSTRUCTION LINE. VERY LIGHT, USED TO CONSTRUCT THE DRAWING, LINE UP PARTS, TRANSFER DIMENSIONS.

B. DIMENSION OR WITNESS LINE. LIGHT, USED TO SHOW THE DISTANCE BETWEEN POINTS. ENABLES A DIMENSION TO BE PULLED AWAY FROM THE LINES OF THE PIECE.

C. LEADER. SAME WEIGHT AS DIMENSION LINE, USED TO SHOW THE PART OF THE DRAWING A NOTE OR LABEL REFERS TO.

D. HIDDEN LINE. MEDIUM AND DASHED, USED TO SHOW PARTS OF THE PIECE THAT ARE HIDDEN BEHIND ANOTHER PART.

E. SOLID INTERIOR LINE. MEDIUM, USED FOR INTERIOR LINES.

F. SOLID OUTLINE. HEAVY, USED TO OUTLINE THE PIECE.

B. drawing techniques

In the early stages of design I tend to work from loose sketches (see p. 6). When the design takes on a more final form, I begin working drawings—either orthographic, isometric or perspective. I find the most useful are orthographic projections—the top, front and end views of an object. Isometric and perspective drawings depict an object more realistically, but orthographic projections most reliably show the true shapes and relationships of parts and the necessary dimensions. I use orthographic projections to determine most of the dimensions of a piece and to work out all construction details.

orthographic projections

In an orthographic projection, each view of the piece is projected onto a flat plane called a picture plane, by lines perpendicular to both the view and the picture plane. It's easiest to imagine this if you visualize the piece enclosed by a glass box; each pane of glass is a picture plane. Note that if a surface of the piece is parallel to a picture plane (A and B in the drawing below), it will be represented true to scale. But if a surface is at an angle to its picture plane (C in the drawing), it will appear foreshor-

**PICTURE PLANES
IN ORTHOGRAPHIC
PROJECTIONS**

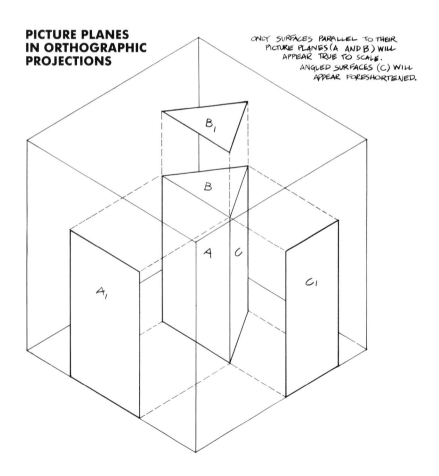

ONLY SURFACES PARALLEL TO THEIR
PICTURE PLANES (A AND B) WILL
APPEAR TRUE TO SCALE.
ANGLED SURFACES (C) WILL
APPEAR FORESHORTENED.

DRAWING ORTHOGRAPHIC PROJECTIONS

Ⓐ START WITH THE TOP (PLAN) VIEW OF THE PIECE.

BASE LINE

Ⓑ THEN ESTABLISH A BASE LINE AND PROJECT DIMENSIONS FROM THE TOP VIEW TO THE FRONT VIEW.

BASE LINE

Ⓒ DEVELOP THE FRONT VIEW WITH INFORMATION NOT GIVEN IN THE TOP VIEW. (THIS WOULD ACTUALLY BE DRAWN OVER THE LINES IN STEP B. THEY HAVE BEEN SEPARATED HERE FOR CLARITY).

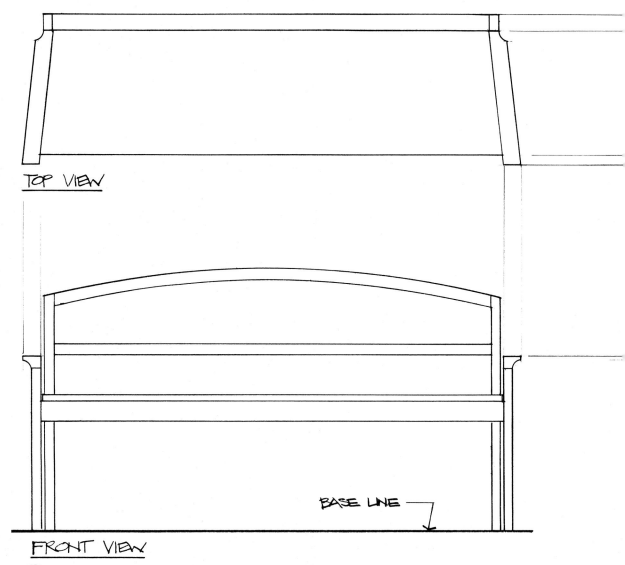

TOP VIEW

FRONT VIEW

BASE LINE

Ⓓ LOCATE THE END VIEW TO THE RIGHT OF THE FRONT VIEW, PROJECTING INFORMATION FROM THE TOP AND FRONT VIEWS.

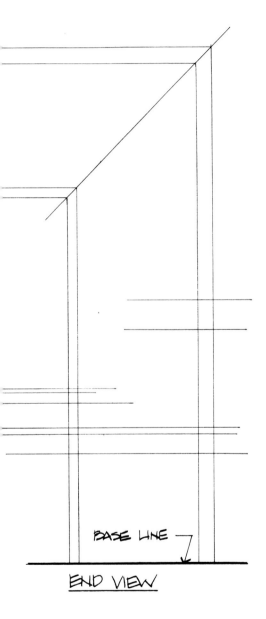

BASE LINE

END VIEW

tened. For accurate dimensions you would have to draw an additional view (J in the drawing on p. 177). The normal orientation of picture planes depicts the top, front and end views of a piece of furniture; each plane is at a 90° angle to adjacent planes. The views of a piece of furniture are usually laid out as if the top edge of the imaginary box were hinged, and the ends and front opened flat.

To begin a set of orthographic projections, first select a convenient scale, based on the piece's complexity and the size of your drawing equipment. I generally let ¼ in. equal 1 in., which allows the top, front and end views of most pieces to be drawn on the same page; this makes it easy to determine the relationship between the views. I do a rough layout to make sure all the views will fit on the page, and that there will be room for dimensioning and notes. I put dimensions on the top and left of the drawings so I don't have to search for them when building the piece, and I place any notes in a column on the right. Full-scale drawings of the entire piece or of selected details can be drawn later if needed, after the form and proportions are determined in the scaled views.

It's a good idea to do several preliminary drawings of one or two views to scale to help develop dimensions, proportions and structure before starting on the final drawings. The view you draw first depends on the piece—picking the one that gives the most essential information makes it easier to develop the other views. Starting with the top (plan) view helps compose the drawing page. Draw this view in the upper left quadrant of the paper, leaving room for dimensions and notes. It is usually difficult to complete the top view without at least beginning to develop the front or end view. The top view may begin as shown at A in the drawing on p. 169.

Next, establish the front view below the top view. Begin by drawing a base line to represent the floor. Using a large triangle, project lines down from the top view to set some of the dimensions in the front view, such as the length of the bench and the location of the legs and armrests (B in the drawing). Then develop the front view further with information not given in the top view, such as seat and backrest height (C in the drawing).

Now locate the end view to the right of the front view (D in the drawing at left). Draw in another base line for the floor. Project lines over from the front view to establish basic dimensions such as seat and backrest height. The width of the bench, along with some other dimensions, can be projected onto the end view from the top view.

TOP VIEW

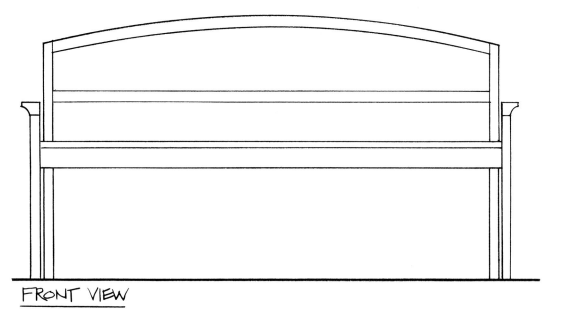

FRONT VIEW

(E) FINISH THE END VIEW BY ADDING NEW INFORMATION AS WELL AS INFORMATION PROJECTED FROM THE TOP AND FRONT VIEWS.

To do this, draw in a 45° construction line above the end view. Then extend construction lines from the top view to the line. At the intersection, continue the lines vertically to the base line of the end view. Finish the end view by using the projected information and by adding new information (E in the drawing at left).

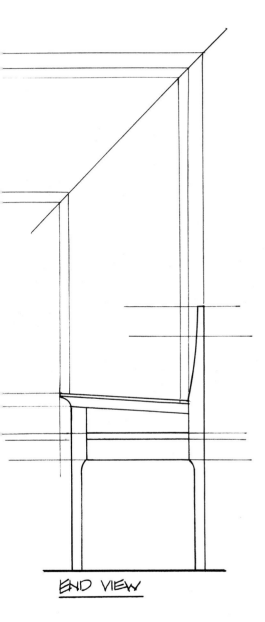

END VIEW

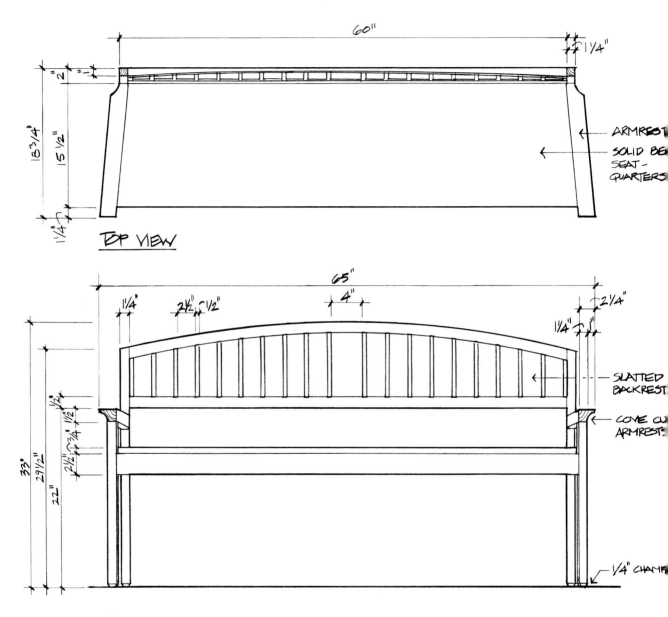

60"

1 1/4"

2"

18 3/4"

15 1/2"

1/4"

ARMREST

SOLID BE
SEAT -
QUARTERS

TOP VIEW

65"

4"

1 1/4"

2 1/2" 1/2"

2 1/4"

1/4"

1/2"

1 1/2"

2 1/2" 3/4"

33"

29 1/2"

22"

SLATTED
BACKREST

COVE CU
ARMRESTS

1/4" CHAMF

FRONT VIEW

BENCH

SCALE: 1/4" = 1"

(F) WHEN THE THREE BASIC VIEWS ARE DEVELOPED, ADD DIMENSIONS
AND CONSTRUCTION INFORMATION. THIS EXAMPLE SHOWS ONLY WHAT
WOULD BE SEEN BY THE EYE (NO HIDDEN LINES).

After the basic forms are created in three views, you're ready to add dimensions and construction information. This step can be simple or complex, according to the level of detail you want. In this example (F in the drawing at left), the bench shows only the information that would be seen by the eye. The drawing gives a good sense of proportion, form and scale, but does not give all the construction information that would be shown in the form of hidden (or dashed) lines.

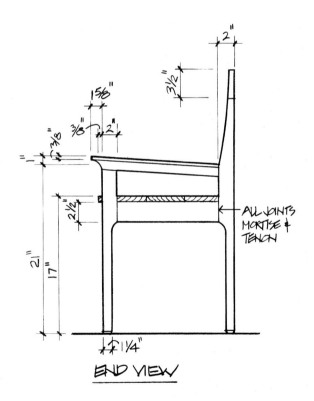

END VIEW

To show structure under the surface, use dashed lines (G in the drawing at right), or draw part of the piece as it would be seen by the eye and part of the piece showing the understructure (H in the drawing on the facing page). At times it will be necessary to draw additional full-scale details (I in the drawing at right) or an entire full-scale view to show all the dimensions and details. Sometimes I draw the top, front and end views of a piece in small scale showing only minimum information and then blow up each view (or part of a view) to give construction information and detailed dimensions.

Remember that any part of the furniture piece that is parallel to a picture plane will be drawn true to scale, but that any part angled away from or toward the plane will not be true to scale. In the case of this bench, the end view of the stretcher is not true to scale because it flares out to the front of the bench. It is therefore not parallel to the plane in which the end view is drawn, but is truly represented in the top view. Here the flare can be seen because the stretcher is parallel to the plane in which the top view is drawn (parallel to the floor plane). The armrest length, however, is not truly represented in either the top or end view, because it both flares out to the front of the bench and tilts down from the front to the back. To draw a view in which the armrest is true to scale, you have to project from the top view an end view that is at right angles to the armrest (J in the drawing on the facing page). But note that all the other horizontal dimensions in this view are then not to scale, because they are angled to the picture plane.

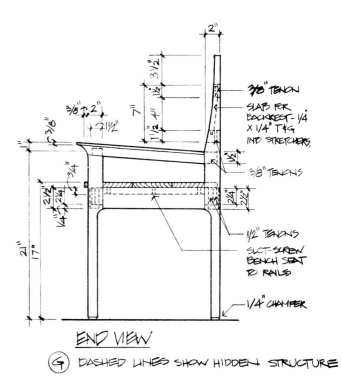

END VIEW

(G) DASHED LINES SHOW HIDDEN STRUCTURE

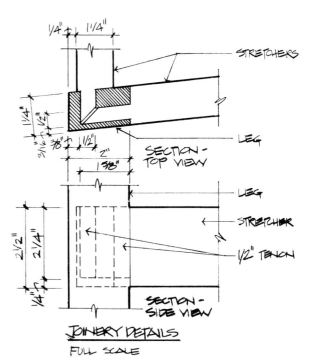

JOINERY DETAILS
FULL SCALE

(I) FULL SCALE DETAILS CLARIFY COMPLICATED AREAS.

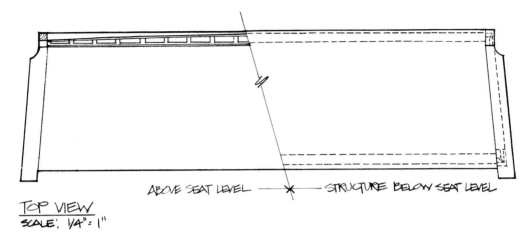

ABOVE SEAT LEVEL ———— X ———— STRUCTURE BELOW SEAT LEVEL

TOP VIEW
SCALE: 1/4" = 1"

(H) ... OR SHOW THIS BY DRAWING PART OF THE PIECE AS IT WOULD
BE SEEN BY THE EYE, PART AS IT WOULD BE BUILT.

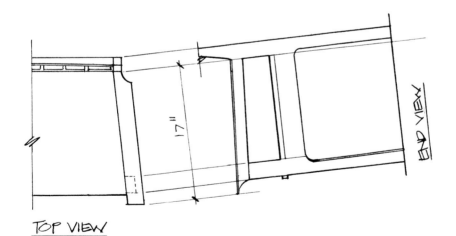

17"

END VIEW

TOP VIEW

PROJECTION DRAWING FOR ARMREST LENGTH
SCALE: 1/4" = 1"

(J) ANY PART OF THE FURNITURE PIECE AT AN ANGLE TO ITS PICTURE
PLANE (SUCH AS THE ARMREST OF THIS BENCH) WILL BE OUT OF
SCALE, BUT CAN BE REDRAWN TRUE TO SCALE AS SHOWN.

isometric drawings

To visualize a design better, I sometimes draw a piece in three dimensions, showing the front, an end and the top, after I complete a set of orthographic projections. An easy way to do this is with an isometric, in which true dimensions are shown on three axes. I usually draw the left and right axes at 30° to the center axis, but the angle can be varied to provide a higher or lower viewing angle. A disadvan-

DRAWING AN ISOMETRIC OF A BENCH

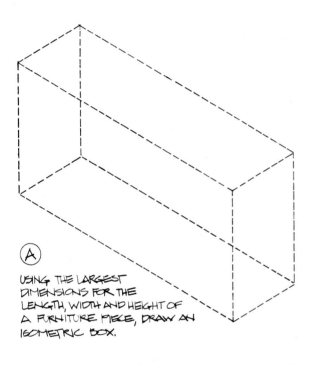

(A) USING THE LARGEST DIMENSIONS FOR THE LENGTH, WIDTH AND HEIGHT OF A FURNITURE PIECE, DRAW AN ISOMETRIC BOX.

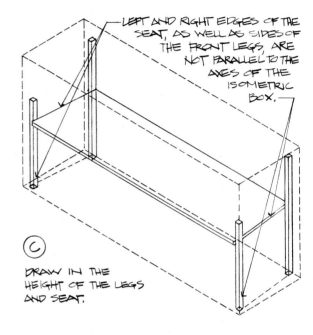

LEFT AND RIGHT EDGES OF THE SEAT, AS WELL AS SIDES OF THE FRONT LEGS, ARE NOT PARALLEL TO THE AXES OF THE ISOMETRIC BOX.

(C) DRAW IN THE HEIGHT OF THE LEGS AND SEAT.

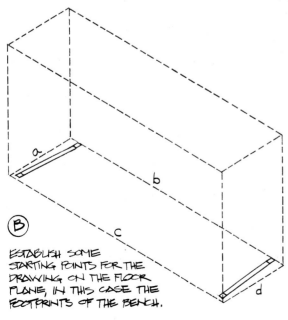

(B) ESTABLISH SOME STARTING POINTS FOR THE DRAWING ON THE FLOOR PLANE, IN THIS CASE THE FOOTPRINTS OF THE BENCH.

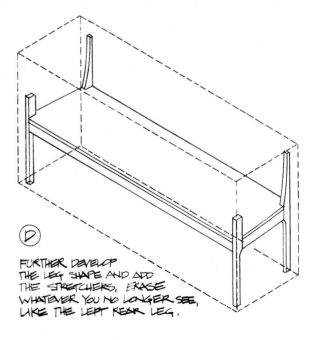

(D) FURTHER DEVELOP THE LEG SHAPE AND ADD THE STRETCHERS, ERASE WHATEVER YOU NO LONGER SEE, LIKE THE LEFT REAR LEG.

tage to isometrics is that, unlike perspective draw-ings (pp. 180-185), they do not illustrate objects the way we truly see them, because lines do not con-verge to represent parts of an object that are farther away from the viewer, but stay parallel infinitely.

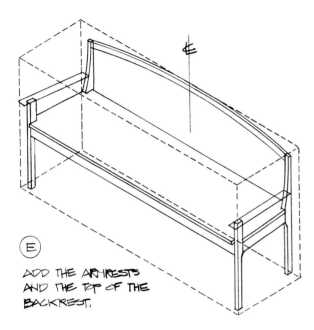

E

ADD THE ARMRESTS
AND THE TOP OF THE
BACKREST.

F

FILL IN THE REST OF THE
BACKREST, DEVELOP THE
ARMREST SHAPE, AND ERASE
THE CONSTRUCTION LINES.

In drawing an isometric of a piece for which there is a set of orthographic projections, start by taking the largest dimensions for the length, width and height. Apply each dimension to an axis to create an isometric box (A in the drawing on the facing page). You then measure other dimensions from this box when drawing the piece. I usually choose a scale of ¼ in. to 1 in. or less. A larger scale is unwieldy and no better in clarifying three-dimensional proportions.

Next, decide on some starting points for the draw-ing. These are usually points that are easy to estab-lish on the floor plane, such as the footprints of the legs (B). These are established by measuring over from lines a, b and d. The armrests of the bench es-tablish the dimension to the front face and the width of the isometric box; they overhang the front legs by 1⅝ in. in the front and 1 in. on the ends, so measur-ing in from lines c, d and a establishes the outer cor-ners of the footprint. Complete the front-leg foot-prints by first locating their width along the front edge, then finding the angle of the footprint sides by connecting lines between the back-leg footprints and the width of the front footprint just established. Finally draw in from measurement the back edge of the front footprint.

Then draw in the height of the legs and locate the seat (C). All these elements have edges parallel to the axes of the isometric box, which means their di-mensions can be drawn true to scale. (Parts of the piece that are not parallel to the axes of the isomet-ric box will not be drawn true to scale.) Just sketch in the legs for reference, but don't show their final shape until the next step (D), at which point you also draw in the stretchers. Erase whatever parts would no longer be visible, like the left rear leg.

The armrests, which slope 1 in. from the front to the back of the bench, come next (E). Since you've drawn the front legs to armrest height, just locate the front of the armrest on top of the front leg. To locate the backs of the armrests, measure along the back edges of the rear legs and then project those points to the front edges of the rear legs to give the proper location. The height of the armrest in front should be 1 in. higher than at the back. Then draw in the top surface of the armrest. This takes the form of a parallelogram, because the armrests flare out toward the front of the bench, and so are not paral-lel to the isometric axes.

At this point also draw in the top stretcher of the backrest. Establish the centerline of the back and then draw in the arched stretcher from the top of the rear legs to the top of this centerline, drawing in the rear top line first. Having fixed the major dimen-sions and points, you are now able to complete the backrest and develop the shape of the armrests (F).

perspective drawings

A perspective drawing portrays an object as it would appear to the eye from a given viewing point. A perspective drawing is created when lines projected from this viewing point intersect a picture plane, as shown in the drawing below.

Selecting the viewing point can be tricky. It requires trial and error and judgment, although to some degree it depends on the kind of object being drawn. For instance, if a chair has a strong front view but an insignificant side view, the viewing point should probably allow the front to remain relatively unangled. In addition, the closer the viewing point is to the object, the more dramatic the drawing will be, but it will also appear distorted. The viewing point can also be varied in height, so the object can be pictured from above or below eye level. A table with an inlaid top may benefit from a high viewing point so the inlay can be seen; a chest of drawers with an unspectacular top may be drawn from a much lower viewing point.

THE PERSPECTIVE VIEW

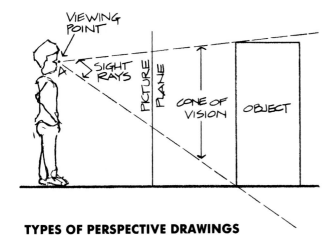

In perspective drawings, lines that in reality are parallel converge to a vanishing point at some distance from the viewer. (In an isometric, these lines stay forever parallel.) The chest shown at left in the bottom drawing has two vanishing points, and is called a two-point perspective. The same chest can be drawn as a one-point perspective, with one vanishing point, as shown at right in the drawing. One-point perspectives are easier to construct but are not used as much as two-point perspectives, so I don't cover them here. It's also possible to construct three-point perspectives, but I have never used them in furniture design.

To construct a two-point perspective, start with a set of orthographic projections (A in the drawing on the facing page). Next, take the top view and choose a viewing point. For furniture, I usually choose a point from which both the front and an end can be seen. Draw a centerline of vision from the viewing point through the top view (B). Then rotate the top view so the centerline of vision is vertical (C). This makes it convenient to lay out the rest of the drawing, since much of the construction to come is parallel or at right angles to the centerline of vision.

Now draw in the cone of vision (D), which simply refers to the angle at which sight rays project from the viewing point. The cone of vision should be symmetrical to the centerline of vision and 45° or less if the object is to appear as it would normally be seen by the eye. If the top view of the object does not fall within the 45° range, move the viewing point farther away.

The next step is to construct a picture plane (E). In the top view, the picture plane is represented as a straight line drawn at right angles to the centerline of vision. The distance that the picture plane is placed from the viewing point determines the size of the perspective drawing. A picture plane in front of the object will produce a small drawing, whereas one drawn behind the object will create a larger image. For this example, the picture plane is placed behind the object. Establish the vanishing points next,

TYPES OF PERSPECTIVE DRAWINGS

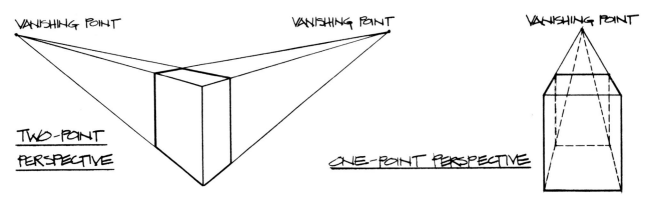

by drawing two lines from the viewing point to the picture plane (F in the drawing on p. 182). These lines are parallel to the piece's front and right end.

Draw in the height line next. Simply project a line from the front, back or one of the ends of the top view until it intersects the picture plane, then extend a vertical line above the picture plane (G in the drawing on p. 182). I usually choose the front of the piece or the end with the most parts or details for the height line (its use will soon become clear).

CONSTRUCTING A TWO-POINT PERSPECTIVE

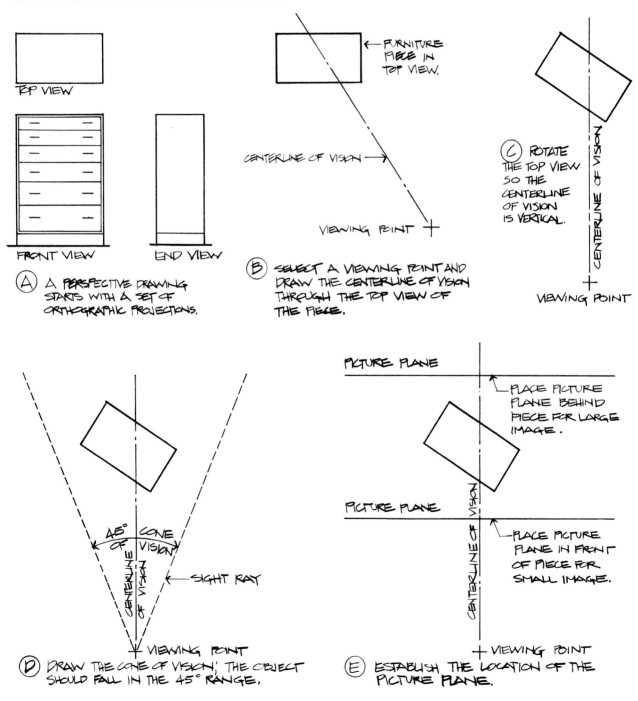

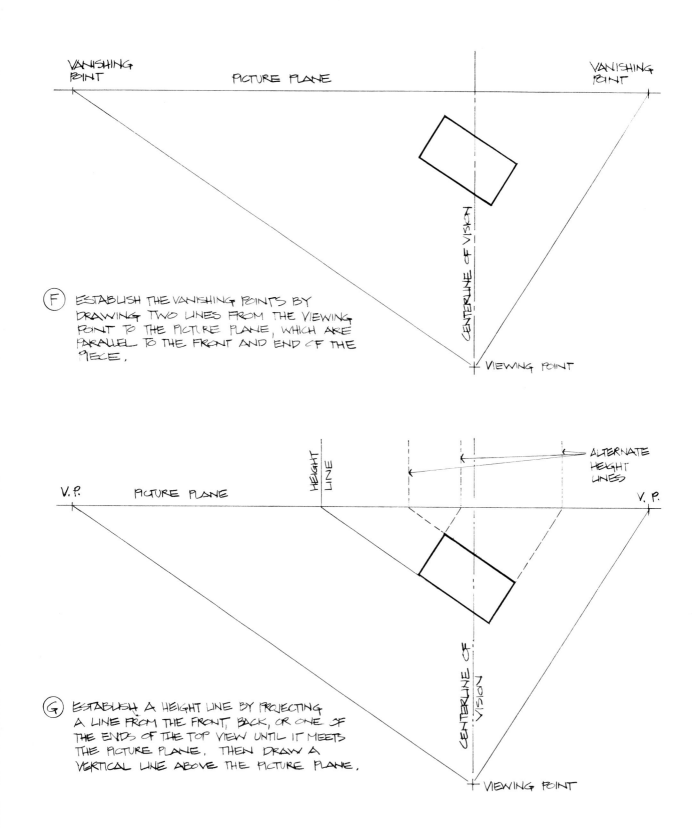

VANISHING POINT

PICTURE PLANE

VANISHING POINT

CENTERLINE OF VISION

F ESTABLISH THE VANISHING POINTS BY DRAWING TWO LINES FROM THE VIEWING POINT TO THE PICTURE PLANE, WHICH ARE PARALLEL TO THE FRONT AND END OF THE PIECE.

VIEWING POINT

V. P.

PICTURE PLANE

HEIGHT LINE

ALTERNATE HEIGHT LINES

V. P.

CENTERLINE OF VISION

G ESTABLISH A HEIGHT LINE BY PROJECTING A LINE FROM THE FRONT, BACK, OR ONE OF THE ENDS OF THE TOP VIEW UNTIL IT MEETS THE PICTURE PLANE, THEN DRAW A VERTICAL LINE ABOVE THE PICTURE PLANE.

VIEWING POINT

All that is left before construction of the perspective is to establish a horizon line and a ground line (H in the drawing below) either above or below the information already drawn. (In this example, I left space above the top view for this purpose.) Assume the floor that the piece sits on is the ground line; when viewing the chest, you would be standing on this line. The horizon line is determined by how high above the ground line the viewing point is meant to be. This is usually 5 ft., which is average

eye level, but it can be higher or lower. Transfer the vanishing points on the picture plane to the same position on the horizon line. These are the points at which the lines of the perspective will converge.

Now construct the drawing. First, measure the height of the object on the height line, from the ground line up (I). This chest is 52 in. high. Second, draw a line from the left vanishing point through the intersection of the ground and height lines. The bottom front edge of the chest will fall at this point,

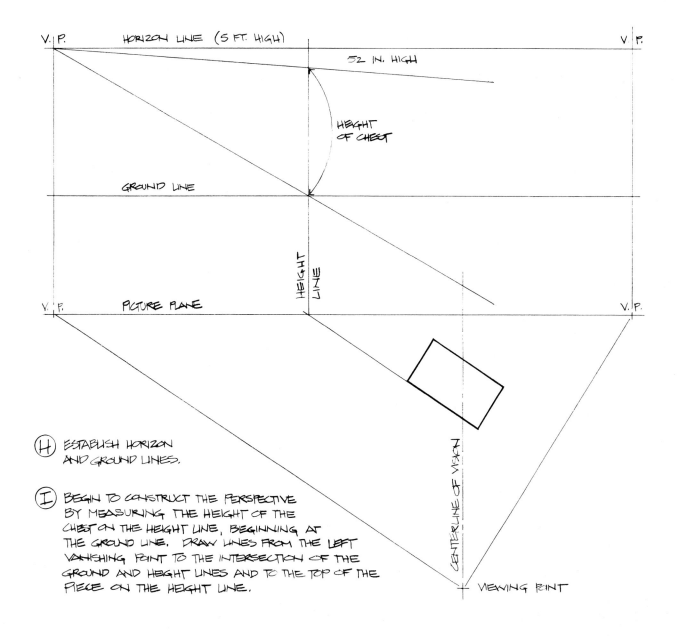

because the height line was generated from the front edge of the chest in top view. Draw a second line from the same vanishing point to the 52-in. mark on the height line. The intersection will form the top front edge of the chest. If you create the height line from the right-hand side of the object, start these lines at the right-hand vanishing point.

From the viewing point, now project lines called sight rays through the corners of the chest on the top view to the picture plane (J in the drawing be-

low). Then vertically project two of these lines, which represent the two front edges of the chest, above the picture plane to intersect the lines just generated from the vanishing points. Connect these lines. This gives the front of the chest in perspective.

Next, complete the outline of the chest by first projecting lines from the right-hand vanishing point to three of the corners of the chest front already drawn (K). Next, lines are vertically projected from the remaining sight rays as shown, and finally the

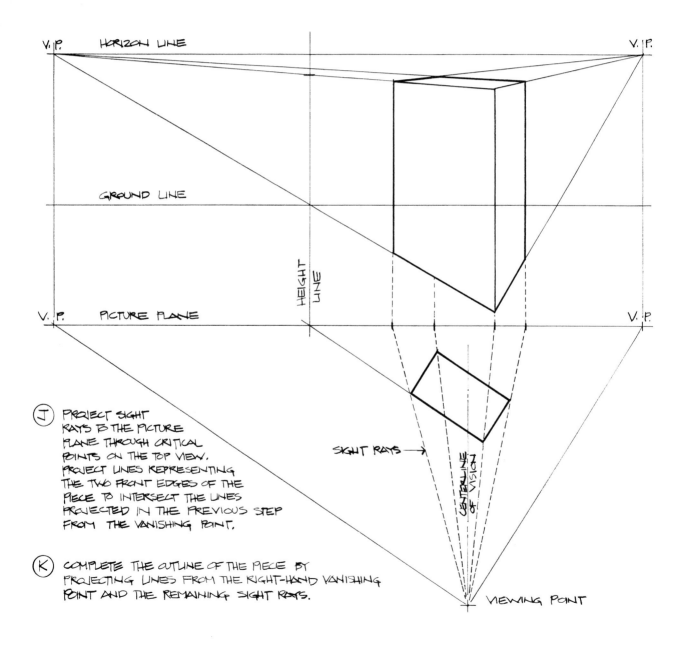

V. P.   HORIZON LINE   V. P.

GROUND LINE

HEIGHT LINE

V. P.   PICTURE PLANE   V. P.

SIGHT RAYS →

CENTERLINE OF VISION

(J) PROJECT SIGHT RAYS TO THE PICTURE PLANE THROUGH CRITICAL POINTS ON THE TOP VIEW. PROJECT LINES REPRESENTING THE TWO FRONT EDGES OF THE PIECE TO INTERSECT THE LINES PROJECTED IN THE PREVIOUS STEP FROM THE VANISHING POINT.

(K) COMPLETE THE OUTLINE OF THE PIECE BY PROJECTING LINES FROM THE RIGHT-HAND VANISHING POINT AND THE REMAINING SIGHT RAYS.

VIEWING POINT

back top edge of the chest is drawn in with a line projected from the left vanishing point to the rear right top corner of the chest. Details within this outline can then be constructed (L in the drawing below). Here I've drawn the front view on the ground line next to the height line so dimensions can easily be projected to the height line. Normally I would just slip a drawing of the front view under the perspective drawing for reference, or I'd simply transfer details to the height line by measurement. By projecting lines from the left vanishing point through these measurements on the height line, you can locate the drawers and hardware on the chest. Locate vertical elements by transferring measurements from the front view to the top view. Then draw lines from the viewing point through these points to the picture plane, and then vertically to the perspective drawing. Again, it usually isn't necessary to redraw the front view of the piece, only to transfer the dimensions by measurement.

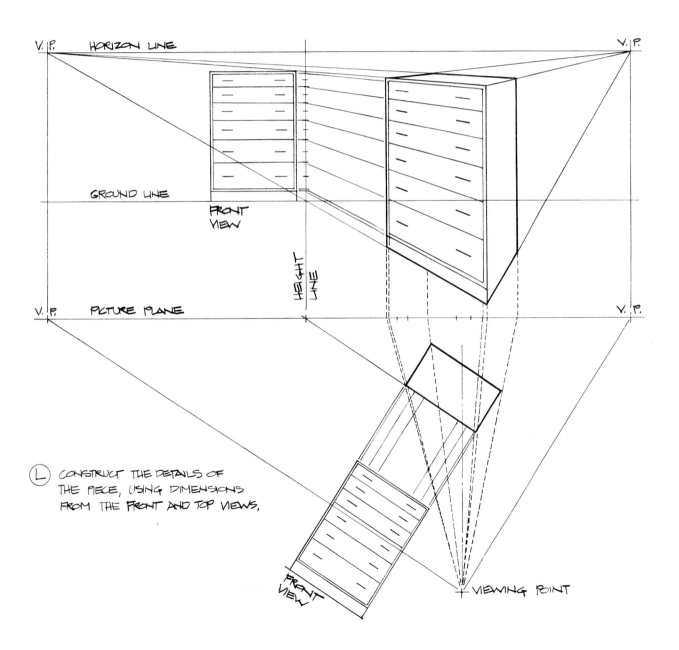

L CONSTRUCT THE DETAILS OF THE PIECE, USING DIMENSIONS FROM THE FRONT AND TOP VIEWS.

C. building models and mockups

Small-scale models are a great way to study designs and to convey information to clients. A surprising number of my clients can't read working drawings, and because I don't have a tremendous talent for sketching and rendering, I usually complement the working drawings of a piece with a model whenever I make a presentation. The complexity of the model depends on the complexity of the design, and many times I've been grateful I took the time to make a study model because of the flaws in form or proportion that it exposed.

A few years ago, when I was making a lot of bentwood furniture, I would usually go right from a quick sketch to models because it was too difficult to draw the shapes I wanted to study. I made most of those models from 12-ga. plastic-coated wire and attached pieces together with hot-melt glue. Most of these were study models and looked sloppy, but they showed forms I couldn't have expressed any other way.

Somewhere between modelmaking and finished working drawings I usually do a full-scale mockup of the entire piece or at least part of the piece. Mockups are useful in further defining forms that have been drawn, such as the shape of a table leg or the edge detail of a stretcher. Mockups also can be used to see scale and proportion first-hand—the size of a chair leg in relation to its stretcher may look good in a scaled orthographic projection, but in full scale and in three dimensions it may look awful. When my students design chairs, I almost always require them to construct a mockup, because this way they can test form, comfort, structure and stability.

models Models can be made of virtually any material—wood, clay, cardboard, wire, paper, metal, plastic or Styrofoam. Select the material according to the size and structure of the model and whether it's a study model for yourself or a finished model for a client. For a study model, you might use inexpensive cardboard held together with tape or hot-melt glue; for a client, you might make a carefully crafted foamcore or illustration-board model. A large, quarter-scale model might warrant wood and Plexiglas parts, whereas a smaller model might be okay with cardboard and acetate.

In my travels I like to pick up scraps of any materials that might come in handy for modelmaking. Still, finding the right material for each new model can be a challenge. I once used some cylindrical ceramic electrical insulators for the legs in a model of a table I was designing—the color and matte finish were perfect. Modelmaking materials can also be found in hobby shops, hardware stores and art-supply stores, as well as through modeling magazines like *Model Railroader* (see the Bibliography on pp. 212-213). For expensive modelmaking materials like foamcore

This painted aluminum chair by Elizabeth Browning Jackson of New York, N.Y., was developed through the use of a small, folded-paper study model. (Photo by Seth Stem.)

materials for modelmaking

adhesives
hot-melt glue
spray adhesive
yellow (aliphatic) glue
white (polyvinyl-acetate) glue
rubber cement
cellulose (household) cement
model-airplane cement
plastic-weld cement (such as
  Plastruct®, used to bond styrene,
  ABS plastic and acrylic)
contact cement
double-sided tape
masking tape
transparent tape

fasteners
brads
wire nails
modelmaking pins (½ in. to
  ⅞ in. long)
screws in small sizes

sheet materials
cardboard
chipboard, $\frac{1}{32}$ in., $\frac{1}{16}$ in. and
  ⅛ in. thick
foamcore, ⅛ in. and $\frac{3}{16}$ in. thick
illustration or mat board, $\frac{1}{16}$ in. thick
museum mounting board, $\frac{1}{16}$ in. thick
paper of all kinds, colors and textures
balsa-wood sheets

Plexiglas, $\frac{1}{16}$ in., ⅛ in. and ¼ in. thick
styrene (plastic that can be formed
  with heat), $\frac{1}{16}$-in. thick sheets
thin sheet aluminum

shaped or solid materials
dowels, $\frac{1}{16}$ in. to 1 in. in dia.
Plasticine® (modelmaker's clay)
basswood, 1 in. and 2 in. thick
plastic or Plexiglas rod (can be
  heat-bent)
balsa wood in strips and shapes
brass and aluminum tubing and rods
  in small sizes
Styrofoam
modeling foam (an expensive, high-
  density foam that retains a high degree
  of detail when cut and shaped)
12-ga. plastic insulated house wire

finishes
Sealers: spray or brush-on shellac
BIN sealer (shellac base, white in
  color, in spray or cans)
wood or metal primer in spray cans
Lacquers: acrylic automotive lacquer
clear lacquer
fast-drying enamels
cold-water, liquid, fiber-reactive dyes
watercolors
black and colored inks
leather dyes
texture paint

miscellaneous
pressure-sensitive tapes in various
  widths and colors
pressure-sensitive films in dots,
  patterns and colors
colored pencils
felt-tip markers
fabric scraps (finer weaves, as in silk,
  are generally more successful because
  they are more in scale with the rest
  of the model)

tools and work surfaces
utility knives (X-Acto, Stanley, Olfa) of
  different sizes for heavy to light work
steel straightedge
papercutter
hot-melt glue gun
pottery-shaping tools (for working
  with modeling clay)
clamps
vise
small needlenose pliers
tweezers
fine-tooth dovetail saw
files and rasps
hand drill and bits
kitchen knife or penknife
rubber bands
⅛-in. thick Masonite, ⅛-in. thick
  chipboard or a rubber cutting pad (as
  cutting bases)

(lightweight polystyrene foam sandwiched between paperboard facings) and good-quality cardboard, you can check picture-framing shops, which often discard quite a bit of usable scrap that can be had for the asking.

Above is a list of materials and tools I find handy for making models. Obviously, you won't need all of these all the time, but I keep many of them on hand.

Following are some examples of study and finished models. For both kinds, it's important to select the scale of the model before starting work. The model should be a manageable size yet still allow an adequate level of detail. When using working drawings (even preliminary ones) as the basis for a model,

reduce them to the right scale either with a photocopier or by redrawing.

For organic shapes having mass and compound-curved surfaces, Plasticine® is a good modelmaking material. Work it with a short knife and pottery-shaping tools. But Plasticine® is so malleable that you can forget other materials will present structural or construction problems. It can be hard or impossible to transfer an interesting form developed in Plasticine® to a piece of furniture, unless you use stack lamination or molded-fiberglass techniques for highly organic or compound-curved forms.

When making a model of a piece having a regular form, where views can be represented through true-

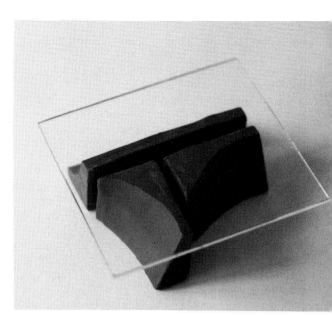

scale orthographic projections, I sometimes make a blackline print or photocopy of the drawings, cut out each view and affix the print to some cardboard or foamcore with spray adhesive. Then I glue all the parts together—the prints can be rendered with markers or colored pencils before or after being attached to the model substrate. Blackline prints work better than photocopies when using markers because the ink of the photocopy may smear when a marker is used over it.

Finished models demand a higher level of skill and more attention to details and finishes. The model at top left on the facing page has foamcore for the main structure and cardboard for the tambour, and both were sprayed with acrylic lacquers. Plastic rods support the Plexiglas writing surface, to which a pressure-sensitive dot grid film was applied to indicate the working areas. Pressure-sensitive tape outlines the drawers and base. This model took six hours to build.

mockups There are no rules for making mockups. I usually make mine out of scrap 2x4s, pine, poplar or basswood, plywood and particleboard. I use as direct a method as possible to assemble the parts—nails, drywall screws and hot-melt glue are my favorite fasteners. I don't necessarily treat the entire mockup with the same degree of attention. For example, if I have a good idea of how a chair leg is going to look, I might not spend as much time on it as on the armrest, where I wish to explore various shapes and test the comfort of each. If possible, use the mockup process to expedite final construction. For example, if you build a tapering jig to make a table leg for the mockup, try to make the jig so it can be used or altered for the finished piece, too.

FACING PAGE, TOP LEFT: This finished model of a tamboured desk was made of foamcore, cardboard, acrylic lacquers, plastic rods, pressure-sensitive dot grid film and pressure-sensitive tape. (Photo by Seth Stem.)

FACING PAGE, TOP RIGHT: This study model is made of Plasticine®, an excellent material for forming curved surfaces. (Photo by Seth Stem.)

FACING PAGE, BOTTOM: A more refined way to make a model is to affix a print of a drawing to a substrate such as cardboard, cut out the shapes of each surface, render with colored pencils or markers, and then glue the pieces together. (Photo by Seth Stem.)

BELOW LEFT: A series of chair mockups was made by Bill Wurz of San Francisco, Calif. In this mockup, Wurz developed his concept of a multi-position chair—the user can sit facing front or sideways, with legs extended over the low armrest. A bentwood strip defines the backrest form, which was intended to receive upholstery. (Photo by Bill Wurz.)

BELOW RIGHT: The piece in this photo was one of the earliest versions, and expressed the asymmetry of form the designer had in mind. It is held together with clamps and drywall screws. Note the temporary support under the seat. (Photo by Bill Wurz.)

In the series of mockups on pp. 189-190, the maker addressed the issues of form, composition, comfort and sitting position. The mockups were quick and direct and used materials at hand—foam rubber and lamination strips that would bend easily and outline the form of the curved backrest areas, which would be upholstered. Changes were made quickly and new options tried out by altering or cannibalizing existing mockups to express the next generation of ideas. (The finished chair is shown on p. 31.)

Sometimes mockups can be turned directly into finished furniture. The advantage to working this way is that you can see the piece develop three dimensionally and in full scale, but sometimes materials are wasted. The table shown on the facing page was designed by this method. Various lengths of the same size stock were milled up and the parts temporarily clamped, tied or glued together to form the structure until the designer arrived at a satisfactory composition and made the structure secure.

BELOW: Wurz's final mockup defined parts of the chair's structure, such as the front legs. Foam rubber simulates the upholstery. In this way, the chair could be tested for comfort as well as appearance. (Photo by Bill Wurz.)

FACING PAGE: This table by Tom Loeser of Cambridge, Mass., was designed without a drawing. The structural elements were composed in full scale and then joined to create the final piece. (Photo by Dean Powell.)

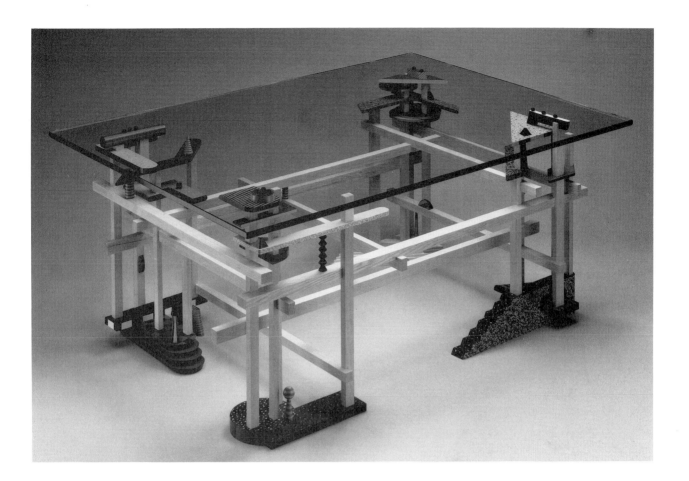

D. putting it all together: designing a piece of custom furniture

Every designer is different, and so is each design project. But I thought it would be useful to beginning designers if they could follow a typical design experience from conceptualization to implementation. Here is the record of a speculative piece of furniture that I designed.

The first question, of course, was what kind of piece to make. As a designer and maker of furniture, I've found that pieces having an unusual function are often especially appealing to prospective buyers, who seem to find it easier to justify the expense of a handcrafted piece if it performs a unique service. The problem statement that I developed, therefore, was to select a piece of furniture with a specialized function that would have appeal as a specialized object. I immediately embarked upon research to identify appropriate objects and to define a concept. I came up with the following list:

— *jewelry boxes and cabinets*. Like the objects they house, these containers are often precious and can command relatively high prices.
— *dressing mirrors*. For some people, dressing up is a daily ritual, to which an elaborate mirror can add much enjoyment.
— *pipe cabinets*. Pipe smoking can fuel the desire to own a special cabinet in which to store a fine collection of pipes.
— *collector's cabinets*. Those who collect objects (from antique guns and butterflies to old woodworking tools) usually appreciate high-quality display cabinets to show off their treasures.
— *accessories for the wine connoisseur*. The rituals of storing, displaying and serving demand expensive furniture to complement the high-priced wine.

I was particularly fascinated with this last category, so I carried my research further by talking to wine merchants and reading books about wine. Initially I thought about designing a grand wine rack, but then in my reading I came across a kind of table I had never heard of before—a decanting table, used in Europe to serve fine red wine. On the top surface, this small table has a cradle that can support a wine bottle horizontally. After a bottle is gingerly carried up from the wine cellar (in the same position as it was stored in the rack, so the sediment will not be disturbed and embitter the wine), it is placed on the decanting-table cradle. A candle is lit underneath, the cork is removed, and the wine is carefully poured into a decanter until the sediment, illuminated by the light of the candle, starts to flow to the bottle's mouth.

Here was a piece of furniture that was definitely specialized. The only problem was that the market would probably be extremely limited. I decided to undertake the project anyway, with hopes that a wine connoisseur would eventually come along who was as intrigued with the piece as I was. My concept therefore became to construct a wine-decanting table that had a precious quality about it. (To my surprise, I found a buyer for the table before I finished writing this book.)

Next, I had to determine the functional requirements of the piece. It needed a cradle at a convenient height, a light source (maybe an incandescent light instead of the candle) and a drawer to hold a corkscrew, napkin, funnel and glass tasting spoon. It also needed a rack or platform to hold the decanter and a small surface on which to put things, such as the cork and corkscrew. For the aesthetic requirements, at this stage I determined that the piece should be made with rich materials and convey elegance. While these criteria would influence my sketches, they would still allow me to experiment with as many different forms as I could imagine.

Now it was time to come up with some ranges of dimensions, as dictated by function. I had to figure out an appropriate cradle height and a shape that would accommodate the different kinds of red-wine bottles. (I learned that a bordeaux bottle has a substantially different shape from a burgundy bottle, and the length of bordeaux bottles varies in both the neck and vessel sections.) I also had to figure out the light intensity necessary to see through green glass and the placement of the decanter on the rack. I studied wine-decanting bottles in several stores, and found that typically bases were no larger than 9 in. in diameter and height ranged from 7 in. to 14 in. With all this in mind, I began to sketch (see the drawing on the facing page).

SOME THUMBNAIL SKETCHES FOR THE WINE-DECANTING TABLE

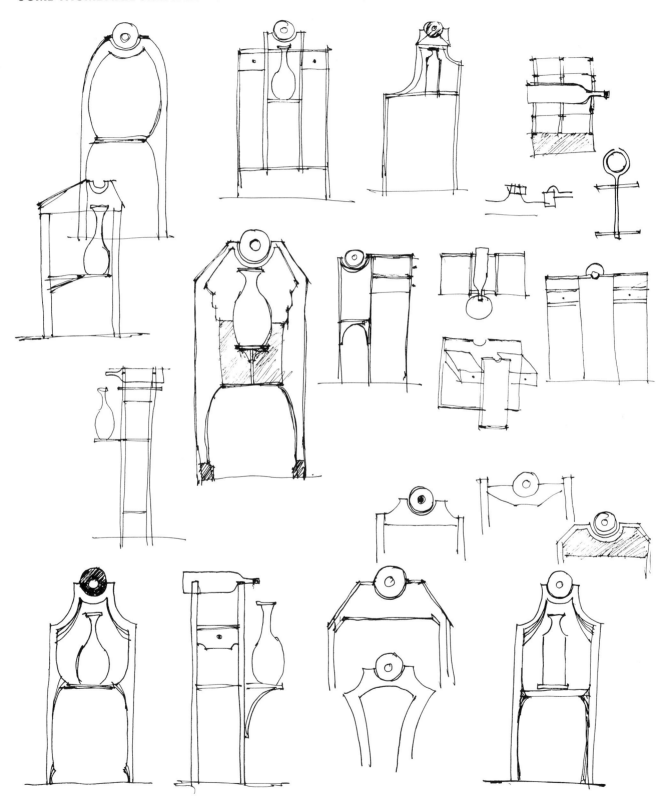

During these early stages of conceptualization and research, it's a good idea to sketch out ideas as fast as they occur—it's common at this point for images of the final piece to flash through your mind with lightning speed. To free myself from preconceived restrictions, my approach to sketching is usually to try to come up with some interesting forms, and then to start blending them with the functional issues. In addition to exploring symmetry versus asymmetry and left-handedness versus right-handedness, in the sketches on p. 193 I looked for pleasing forms and detailing. I can often sketch all my initial ideas in about 30 minutes to an hour. Then I usually need to start some three-dimensional exploration through models or mockups, or to find some additional input by way of a visual reference or icon.

I selected what I thought was the best idea from the sketches and prepared to explore its form through a quick study model. But first I had to get the piece into scale and see its proportions, at least generally. Using the dimensions for bottle size and cradle height that I gathered in my research, I made a simple scaled drawing of the front and side views, which is shown below.

I then began work on the study model (shown in the top photo on the facing page), using foamcore because it cuts into curves easily yet has enough strength to be self-supporting. When the model was finished, I realized that the table was too shallow (front to back) both for the height of the piece and to support the act of opening the wine bottle. I returned to the drawing board.

It was difficult to increase the depth of the table because the design responded so directly to the length of a wine bottle. And adding a front leg under the decanter rack for stability didn't look right. I tried a few new sketches and generated two additional structures that would solve the problems of the previous alternative. After quickly creating a set of scaled drawings for each, I started in on full-scale mockups (bottom photos, facing page), using 2x4s and some pine I had around the shop. Using a hot-

TWO SIMPLE SCALED VIEWS

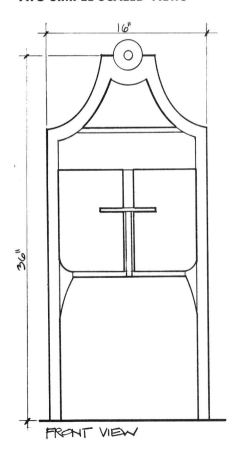

FRONT VIEW

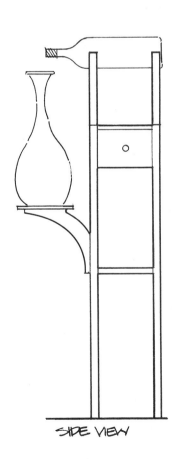

SIDE VIEW

melt glue gun for assembly, it took me only slightly longer to make the mockups than it would have to put together some models, and I could really tell how things looked and worked. The symmetry of the new designs allowed the piece to be used by either a right-handed or a left-handed person. When I decanted a bottle of wine, I found both structures

RIGHT: A foamcore study model revealed that the piece lacked enough depth (front to back) for both visual appeal and opening wine bottles. (Photo by Seth Stem.)

BELOW: Both the second and third mockups (shown here) worked well, but Stem preferred the look of the one at right and chose it to develop. Pine scraps, 2x4s and hot-melt glue were used as construction materials. (Photos by Seth Stem.)

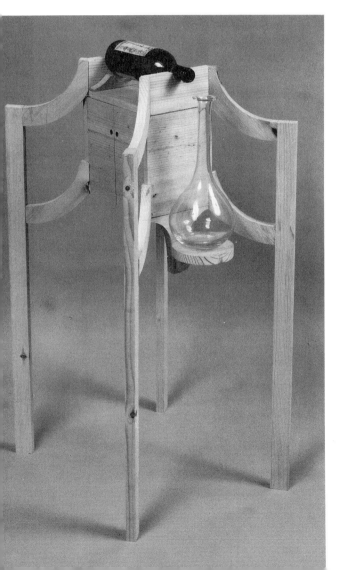

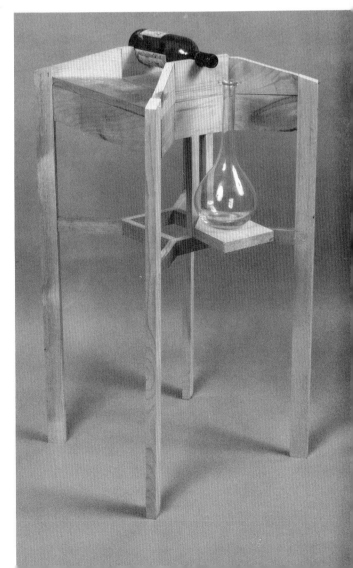

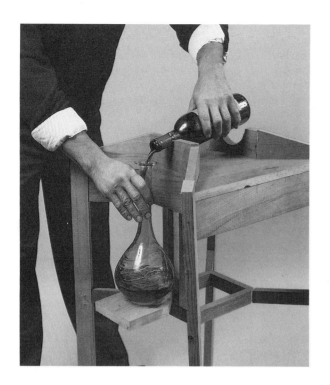

were stable, but I preferred the second option, shown at bottom right on p. 195. I gave up the notion of a drawer on either side of the decanting cradle, however, because a straight-sided drawer would not use the space effectively and a wedge-shaped drawer would be too hard to track. I decided that two compartments with lids would be an acceptable solution. The new design definitely seemed to call for an incandescent light source in the center between the two storage compartments, rather than a candle.

Although I was satisfied with the form and structure of the last design, I felt I needed some aesthetic direction. I had already decided that the piece should be elegant, so whimsical forms were out. But should it have a sleek, modern look—should it be made of steel and glass or marble and silver plate? Or should it be quiet—serviceable and conservative, yet warm and inviting? I chose the latter option and decided to use wood for the structure, both for its warmth and for its traditional value. Still, I needed a visual reference to help with the overall character of the piece and its detailing.

A visual reference need not necessarily relate in any way to the object under design. For example, a

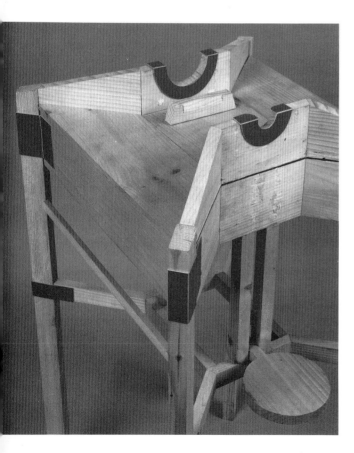

ceramic vessel may be the point of inspiration for the shape of a table leg. In this case, however, I thought it would be fun to try to bring in some way the rich visual vocabulary of winemaking to the table. Vineyards and grape presses came immediately to mind. When I visited a local winery, I was struck by the rows and rows of oak barrels used for aging wine. I especially liked the way the steel bands held the barrel staves together, and that was the image I used for a visual reference.

I abstracted the steel barrel bands into much smaller clip forms for detailing the joint areas. Again using hot-melt glue, I cut out and applied pieces of cardboard to the mockup (photo facing page, bottom left), trying various sizes and shapes, peeling off one attempt and gluing on another. I also used these clip forms to help define the cradle area. The detailing elevated the piece from plainness (vin ordinare) to a visually active appearance (grand cru), which seemed in keeping with the character of the piece I was trying to create. After I was satisfied with the general look, I did a study of different combinations of wood and built a quick mockup of a leg section in walnut with rosewood accents (photo facing page, bottom right). The dark hues conveyed richness without flamboyance, and the two colors were harmonious—more contrast would have made the banding details too busy. Walnut was also a reasonable choice from the standpoint of construction. A harder wood, such as maple or purpleheart, would have taken longer to work.

One of the nice things about doing a mockup is that you can evaluate all aspects before building the actual piece. In the end, I decided not to use the rosewood to define the bottoms of the legs as I had originally planned, because I felt rosewood feet would compete with the upper area of the piece, which I wanted to be dominant. The line weight (visual width) of the parts also seemed satisfactory, with one exception. I wanted to make the legs slightly thicker so they would be noticeably different from the stretcher width.

Having decided on materials, structure and detailing, I did a final working drawing to help in construction and to resolve as many loose ends as possible. I referred to the mockup to establish final dimensions, especially in the area that holds the wine bottle and decanting accessories. At this time, I decided that the lidded compartments should hold two wine glasses along with the other accessories. After checking the size of these implements I realized the compartments were cramped, so I widened them slightly and put in some bars on the outside to hold the napkins. I then brought the top, front and end views to as complete a state as possible.

I hadn't yet resolved the small shelf to hold the decanter. I knew it should be adjustable to accommodate all sizes of decanters, because the mouth of the decanter has to be right under the mouth of the wine bottle when pouring. I did some sketches of various adjustment mechanisms and then a mockup of the solution, which seemed to work fine. I then did a full-scale working drawing of the detail.

I also had to figure out the position of the napkin bars. When I experimented on the mockup, I didn't like the way they looked because the bars hit the legs at an angle, which seemed awkward. I then sketched other ways the bars and legs might work together (similar to the line/circle interaction explained on p. 74). Where the bars hit the face of the leg seemed arbitrary, and it was hard to relate edges to edges or lines to lines. The best solution seemed to be the one in the center of the drawing below, because the back edge of the leg lined up with the flared angle at the end of the bar, and because the

---

FACING PAGE, TOP: The design proved stable during use. (Photo by Seth Stem.)

FACING PAGE, BOTTOM LEFT: Cardboard pieces on the mockup, attached with hot-melt glue, gave the flexibility to experiment with the location and sizes of the banding details. (Photo by Seth Stem.)

FACING PAGE, BOTTOM RIGHT: The combination of walnut and rosewood conveys a subtle richness that complements the banding details. (Photo by Seth Stem.)

A FEW OPTIONS OF LEG AND NAPKIN-BAR ATTACHMENT

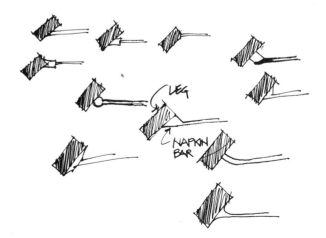

outer face of the bar was in line with the opposite edge of the leg. I still wasn't totally happy with the solution, so I decided to think about it some more.

Because the decanting table would probably be moved around, more than likely from the side of a room to the dining-table area, I felt that a light source requiring a cord and outlet would be impractical. I had planned for a small space underneath the wine bottle for the light, and at this time went shopping to make sure I could find a small, powerful light that would fit. I wound up buying a small, battery-powered halogen flashlight at a local electronics-supply store, along with a switch, battery holder and wire, and I adapted some of the flashlight parts into the lighting arrangement I needed.

Finally I began to construct the piece. I selected the walnut from several boards, taking care to match the colors and using riftsawn grain as much as possible to keep the piece looking refined. (Riftsawing produces a close, straight-grain pattern.) I built the piece as it was drawn, not feeling the need to make changes as it reached completion. Putting off the decision about the napkin bars paid off, because during construction I thought of connecting them to the stretchers with small rosewood brackets, thereby avoiding a connection to the legs. On the mockup I tried different placements of the brackets, marked

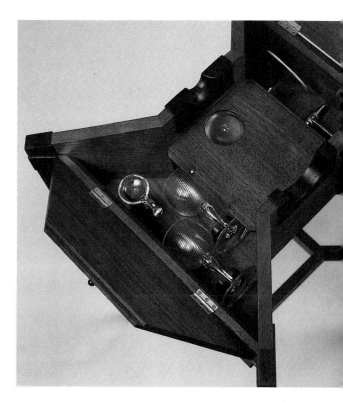

their final position and then mortised the stretchers to receive them. I never drew them on the working drawings, and this omission proved to be a mistake.

After the piece was completed (see the photos on the facing page), I took a few moments to think about what might have been done differently or improved. One of the disappointing details turned out to be the placement of the small rosewood brackets that hold the napkin bars. I mortised the stretchers for them before the table was assembled, having judged their position from the mockup. But the length of the band detail in the mockup was different from the final piece, and therefore the end of each band and the inside edge of each bracket didn't line up (photo below). The discrepancy was especially noticeable because rosewood was used for both the banding and the brackets. I saw the mistake as soon as I went to glue the bars in. Had I taken the time to put the information on the working drawings, I could have determined the proper relationship.

Another part of the design I would improve is the rosewood detailing of the wine cradle. If I had made it larger, particularly on the front and back as shown in the sketch at right, it could have accentuated the prominence of the wine cradle, and would have been more in balance with the plain face of the walnut structure with which it interfaces.

AN ALTERNATIVE WINE-CRADLE DETAIL

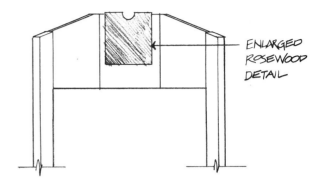

ENLARGED ROSEWOOD DETAIL

FACING PAGE: At left, the wine-decanting table is completed. At right it is shown with its compartments open and the implements they were designed to contain. (Photos by Seth Stem.)

BELOW: The end of the vertical rosewood bracket doesn't line up with the edge of the rosewood napkin bar—an avoidable mistake, had revisions been noted on the working drawings. (Photo by Seth Stem.)

The drawings in this chapter can be used as a general guide to furniture dimensions. In some cases they are an average; in others they are a range. Dimensions for tables and seating are for people of average build (about 68.8 in. tall and 172 lb. for men and 63.6 in. tall and 145 lb. for women). Make adjustments for smaller or larger people. *Humanscale 1/2/3* (see the Bibliography on pp. 212-213) is an excellent source of anthropometric information. Its scales and charts give design dimensions for the average person as well as a range of dimensions for people who fall outside the average.

upholstered lounge seating As shown in the drawings on pp. 200-202, the dimensions of upholstered lounge furniture such as sofas and chairs are quite variable. Seat and armrest heights of sofas should be considered together so the armrest won't be too high above the seat, unless the armrest will be primarily to lean upon. If the chair or sofa is being designed for a small person, reduce the typical seat depth (21 in. to 22 in.) so the front edge won't hit the back of the leg at the knee, which forces short people to slouch forward. Upholstered seats generally slope 1 in. from front to back.

STANDARD DIMENSIONS OF AN UPHOLSTERED CHAIR

STANDARD DIMENSIONS OF A LOVESEAT

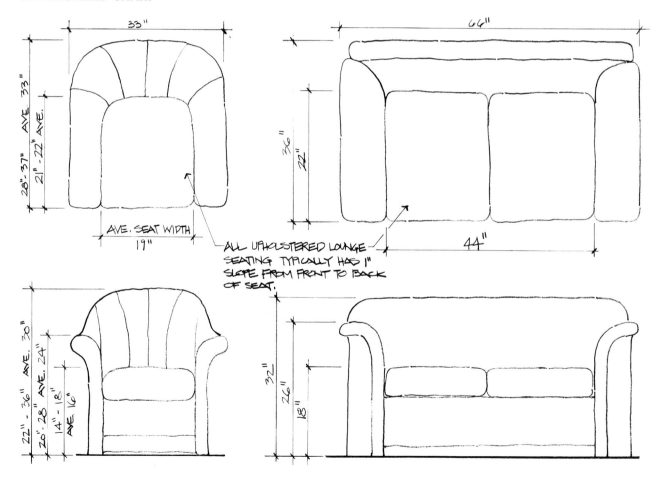

STANDARD DIMENSIONS OF AN APARTMENT-SIZE SOFA

STANDARD DIMENSIONS OF A SECTIONAL SOFA

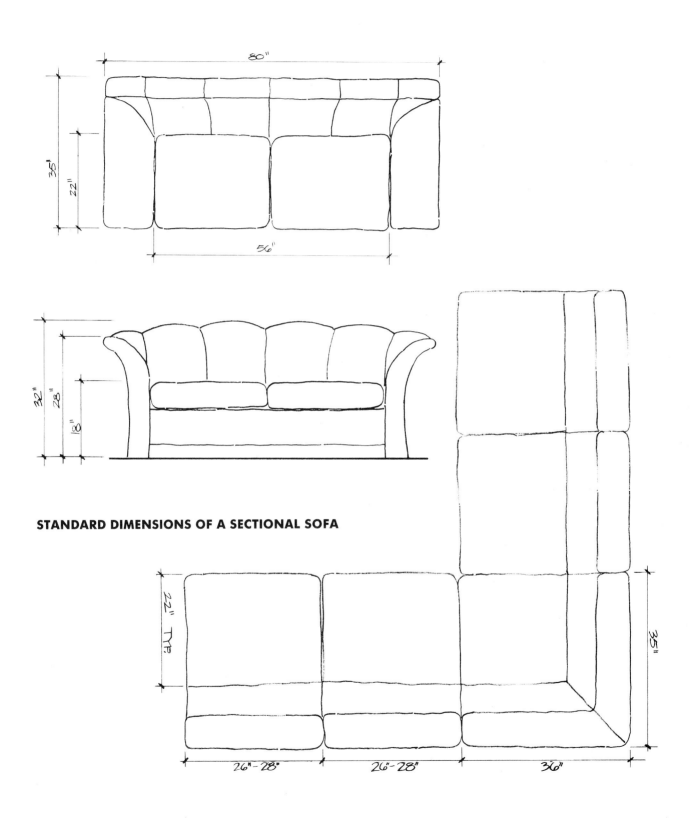

chairs Chair seats range from 14 in. to 19 in. high, the average being 16 in. to 17 in. Seat height relates directly to the slope of the seat and the angle of the backrest—the more the seat is angled, the lower the seat and the greater the backrest angle. (The seat angle should not cause the knee to bend more than 90°.) On padded chairs, consider the compressibility of the padding when determining seat height. Seats are generally slightly wider when armrests are included to allow adequate space for sitting. Seats should be as deep as possible but no longer than the length of the thigh (from the inside of the knee to the back). Refer to *Humanscale 1/2/3* for more detail on seat and back configurations.

STANDARD DIMENSIONS OF A FULL-SIZE SOFA

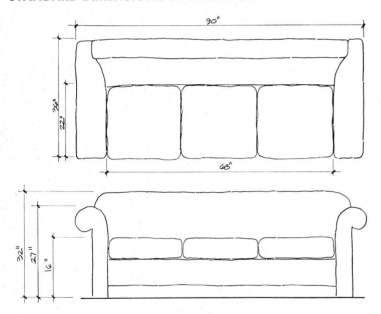

STANDARD DIMENSIONS OF A SOFA WITH CUSHIONS

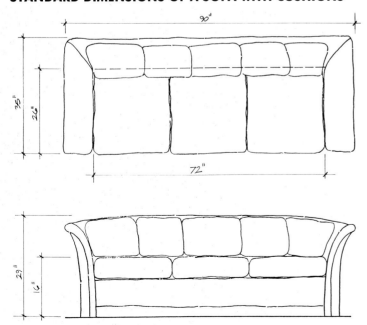

STANDARD DINING-CHAIR DIMENSIONS

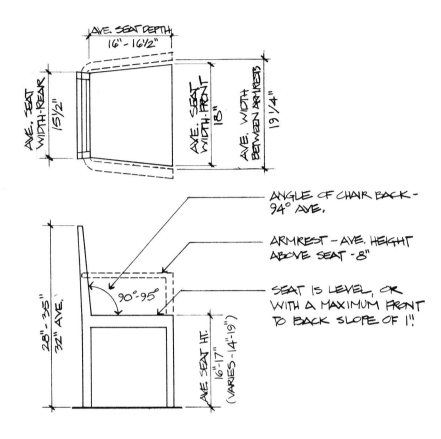

AVE. SEAT DEPTH 16"-16½"
AVE. SEAT WIDTH-REAR 15½"
AVE. SEAT WIDTH-FRONT 18"
AVE. WIDTH BETWEEN ARMREST 19¼"

ANGLE OF CHAIR BACK - 94° AVE.

ARMREST - AVE. HEIGHT ABOVE SEAT - 8"

SEAT IS LEVEL, OR WITH A MAXIMUM FRONT TO BACK SLOPE OF 1"

90°-95°

28"-35" 32" AVE.

AVE. SEAT HT. 16"-17" (VARIES - 14"-19")

STANDARD SEAT/BACK RELATIONSHIP ON A LIGHTLY UPHOLSTERED OR NON-UPHOLSTERED CHAIR

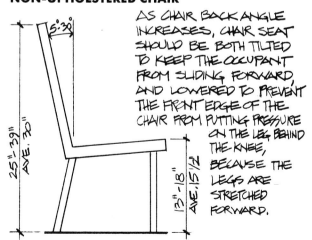

5°-30°

25"-39" AVE. 30"

13"-18" AVE. 15½"

AS CHAIR BACK ANGLE INCREASES, CHAIR SEAT SHOULD BE BOTH TILTED TO KEEP THE OCCUPANT FROM SLIDING FORWARD, AND LOWERED TO PREVENT THE FRONT EDGE OF THE CHAIR FROM PUTTING PRESSURE ON THE LEG BEHIND THE KNEE, BECAUSE THE LEGS ARE STRETCHED FORWARD.

STANDARD ROCKING-CHAIR DIMENSIONS

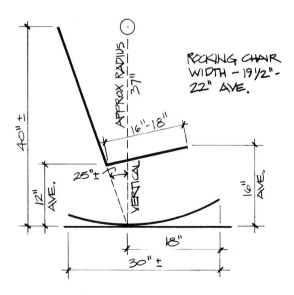

ROCKING CHAIR WIDTH - 19½"-22" AVE.

APPROX RADIUS 37"

16"-18"

40" ±

25° ±

VERTICAL

12" AVE.

16" AVE.

18"

30" ±

DINING-TABLE/CHAIR RELATIONSHIP

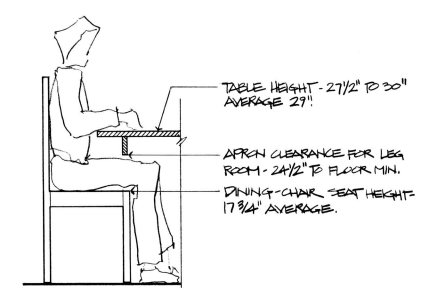

TABLE HEIGHT - 27½" TO 30" AVERAGE 29"

APRON CLEARANCE FOR LEG ROOM - 24½" TO FLOOR MIN.

DINING-CHAIR SEAT HEIGHT- 17¾" AVERAGE.

STANDARD DIMENSIONS OF A TRESTLE TABLE

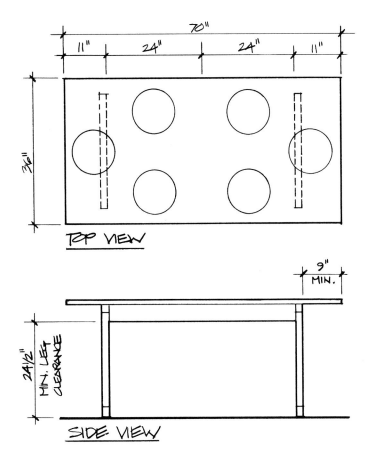

70"

11"   24"   24"   11"

36"

TOP VIEW

9" MIN.

24½" MIN. LEG CLEARANCE

SIDE VIEW

dining tables Heights of dining tables range from 27½ in. to 30 in., depending on the seat height of the chairs, the size of the users and the desired feeling while dining. The height of a tabletop has a tremendous impact on how a person relates to the dining experience. Generally, the higher the surface, the more formal and uncomfortable the table feels. I prefer tables that are lower than the typical 29 in. because they encourage relaxation. I can rest my arms on the top more comfortably, and my viewing angle of the surface is improved.

AVERAGE DIMENSIONS OF ROUND TABLES

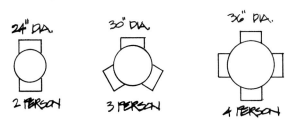

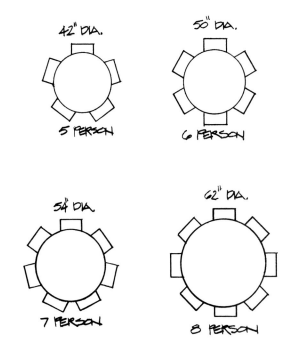

AVERAGE DIMENSIONS OF SQUARE AND RECTANGULAR TABLES

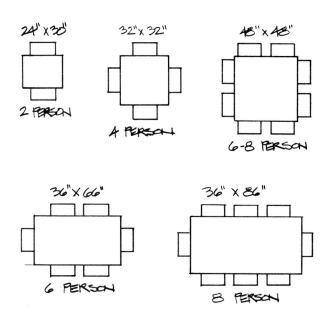

Allow 24-in. width per person for comfortable seating.

Allow 22-in. width per person for snug seating.

	number of people	minimum (in.)	average (in.)	large (in.)
square tables	2	24x24	28x28	30x30
	3-4	30x30	32x32	36x36
	6-8	44x44	48x48	52x52
rectangular tables	2	22x28	24x30	28x32
	4	28x44	32x48	36x52
	6	34x50	36x66	42x72
	8	34x72	36x86	42x90

Allow 26-in. width per person along perimeter for comfortable seating (28 in. for armchairs). Allow 24-in. width per person for snug seating.

Circumference = 3.14 x diameter. To approximate tabletop diameter, multiply the number of seating spaces by 26 in. and divide by 3.14 for three to six people. For more than six people, multiply by 24 in., because the curvature of the table edge decreases.

number of people	minimum dia. (in.)	average dia. (in.)	large dia. (in.)
2	22	24	28
3	28	30	36
4	32	36	42
5	36	42	45
6	42	50	54
7	49	54	62
8	56	62	72

CHILDREN'S FURNITURE— STANDARD DIMENSIONS

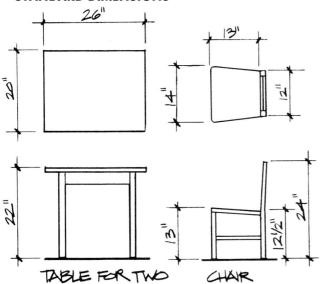

TABLE FOR TWO   CHAIR

occasional tables Occasional tables vary in size and height according to their intended use (coffee table, end table, hall table, etc.), and their relationships to the other furniture pieces in the setting.

dining-room storage Consider building dining-room storage pieces in sections, which fit more easily through doorways when moving. A hutch usually has open shelves or doors on the upper section; a china cabinet usually has glass fronts and sides in its upper section for display.

bedroom furniture Bedside tables should never be more than 6 in. higher than the height of the bed. (Consider whether or not a boxspring will be used.) Bureau dimensions vary tremendously according to style and to the kind of furniture profile desired within the bedroom. Blanket chests are typically 16 in. to 20 in. tall, 36 in. to 54 in. long and 14 in. to 22 in. wide.

STANDARD DIMENSIONS OF OCCASIONAL TABLES

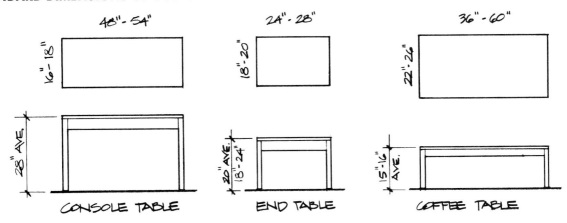

CONSOLE TABLE   END TABLE   COFFEE TABLE

NOTE: COFFEE TABLE HEIGHTS CAN VARY FROM 12" MIN. TO 18" MAX.

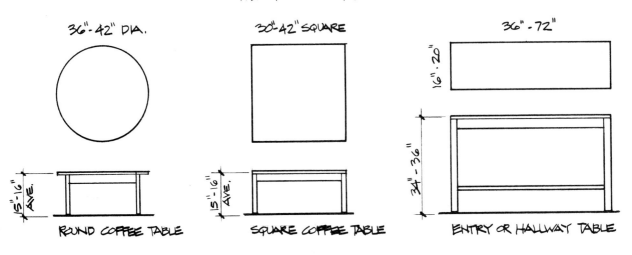

ROUND COFFEE TABLE   SQUARE COFFEE TABLE   ENTRY OR HALLWAY TABLE

STANDARD DIMENSIONS OF DINING-ROOM STORAGE UNITS

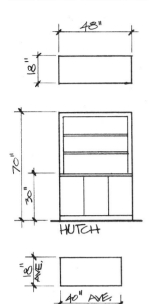

HUTCH

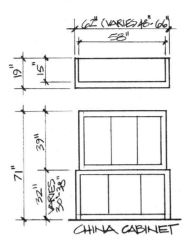

CHINA CABINET

SIDEBOARD

STANDARD DIMENSIONS OF SOME BEDROOM FURNITURE

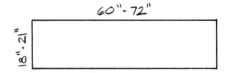

DRESSER OR BUREAU

CHEST OF DRAWERS

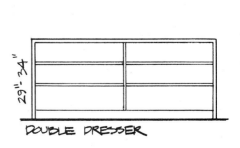

DOUBLE DRESSER

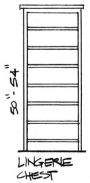

LINGERIE CHEST

STANDARD DIMENSIONS OF A DOUBLE BED

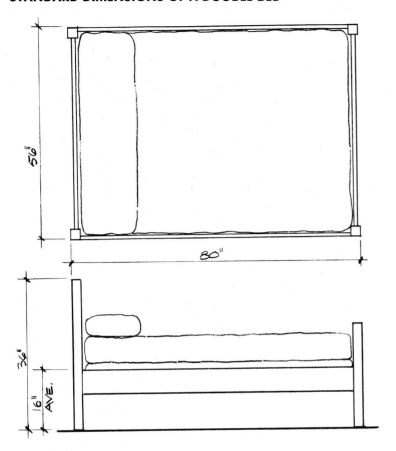

ALLOW 1" TO 2" BETWEEN MATTRESS AND FOOTBOARD FOR HEAVY BEDCLOTHES TO BE TUCKED IN.

5'6"

80"

36"

16" AVE.

STANDARD MATTRESS HEIGHT WITH BOXSPRING

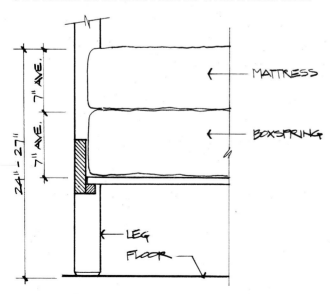

24" – 27"

7" AVE.

7" AVE.

7" AVE.

MATTRESS

BOXSPRING

LEG

FLOOR

STANDARD MATTRESS HEIGHT WITHOUT BOXSPRING

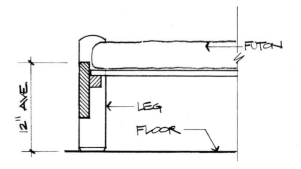

12" AVE.

FUTON

LEG

FLOOR

beds Because mattress sizes vary slightly from manufacturer to manufacturer, it is best to measure the mattress to be used before building the bed or crib. Typical mattress sizes are 36 in. by 75 in. for a single; 39 in. by 75 in. (or 80 in.) for a twin; 54 in. by 75 in. (or 80 in.) for a double; 60 in. by 80 in. (or 84 in.) for a queen; and 76 in. by 80 in. (or 84 in.) for a king. A crib mattress is usually 27 in. by 54 in. Leave 2 in. to 3 in. at the end of the bed if the design includes a footboard, so heavy bedclothes can be tucked in. Bed heights vary—those shown in the drawing are average.

Futons are usually made the same length and width as standard boxsprings and mattresses. They vary in thickness from 3 in. to 6 in.

STANDARD CRIB AND CRADLE DIMENSIONS

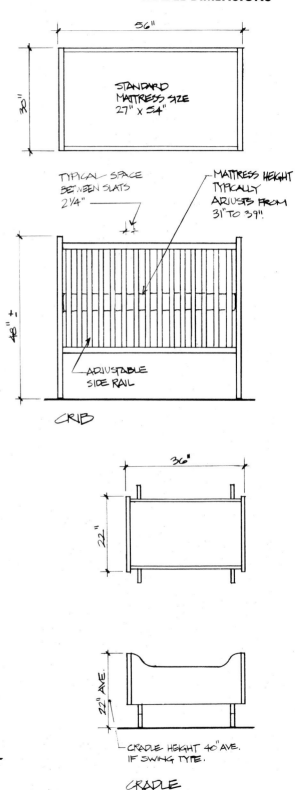

STANDARD BUNK-BED DIMENSIONS

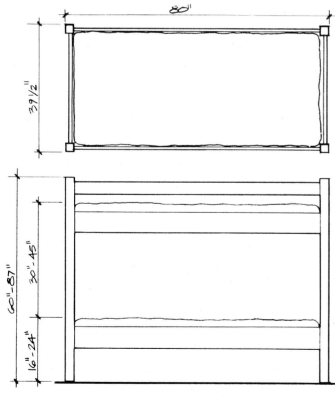

office furniture In past decades, tremendous effort has gone into the design of office furnishings, with adaptability, the handling of telephone and computer wires and systems for open office plans as primary considerations. The dimensional information given here therefore is extremely rudimentary.

When designing office desks, consider how the desk presents the person working behind it (large scale and mass, for instance, convey prestige and power), and consider that in many situations clients or co-workers sit on the opposite side of the desk, so that a modesty or privacy panel may be necessary.

STANDARD DIMENSIONS OF OFFICE WORK STATIONS

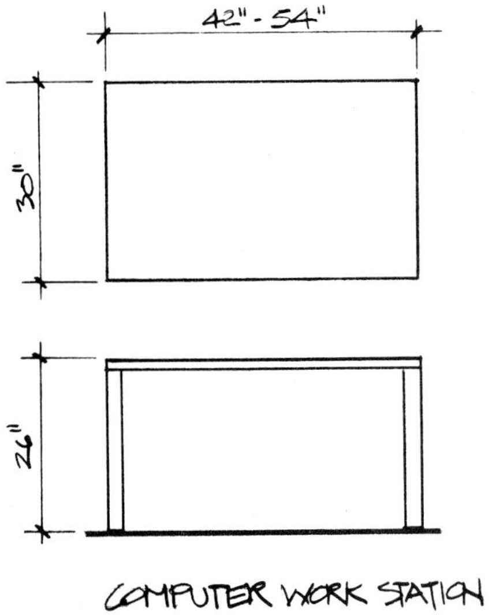

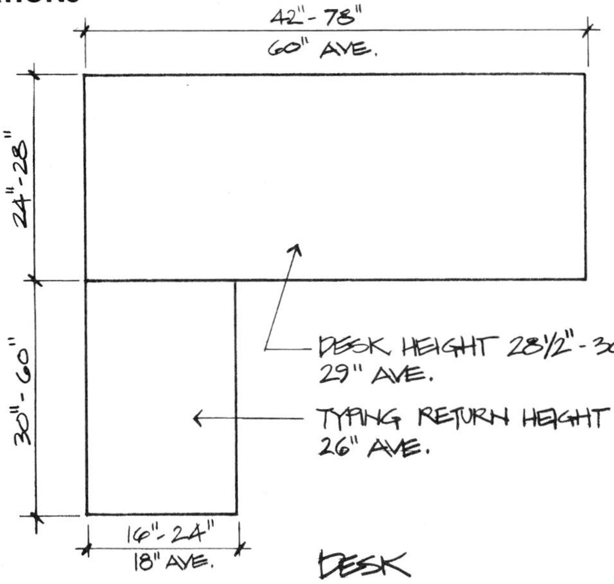

COMPUTER WORK STATION

DESK

DESK HEIGHT 28½"-30", 29" AVE.

TYPING RETURN HEIGHT 26" AVE.

BOOKSHELF

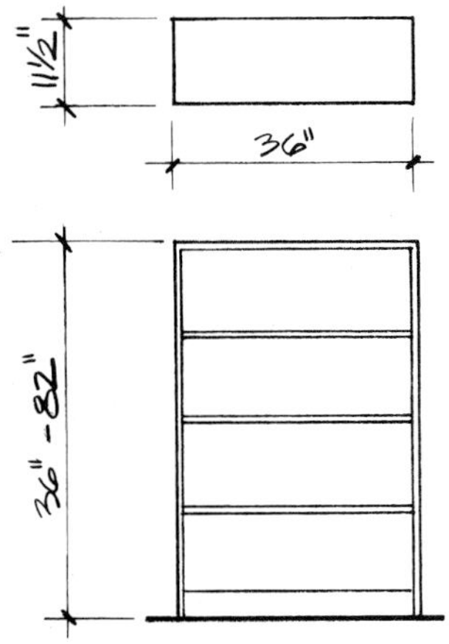

OFFICE CREDENZA

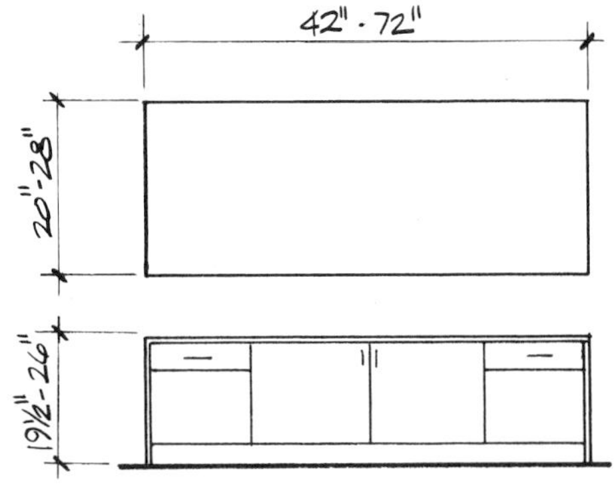

FILE CABINETS

2 DR. LETTER
W 15"
H
D

2 DR. LEGAL
W 18"
H 28"
D 22"-28"

4 DW. LETTER
W 15"
H 52¼"
D 26⅜"-28"

4 DW LEGAL
W 18"
H 52¼"
D 26⅝"-28"

WRITING DESK

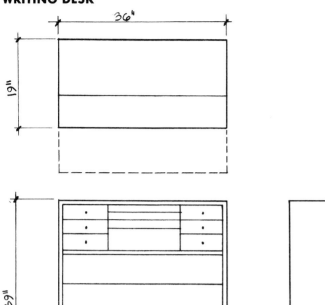

The maximum span of bookshelves in a bookcase depends largely on the materials used—solid hardwood can span greater distances than particleboard or plywood. Generally, shelf spans over 36 in. in hardwood and 30 in. in plywood or particleboard should be supported by dividers if heavy loads will be borne unless facings or other structural elements are incorporated to increase shelf strength.

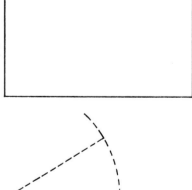

DRAFTING TABLES

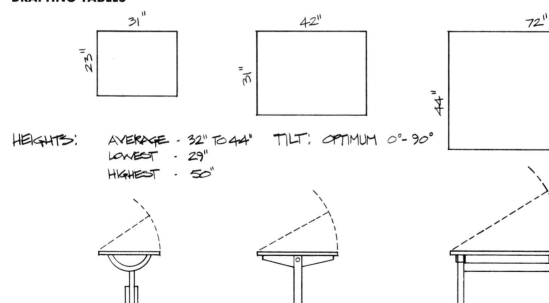

HEIGHTS: AVERAGE - 32" TO 44"   TILT: OPTIMUM 0°-90°
LOWEST - 29"
HIGHEST - 50"

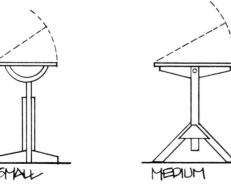

SMALL   MEDIUM   LARGE

bibliography

books

Baroni, Daniele. *The Furniture of Gerrit Rietveld.* Woodbury, N.Y.: Barron's Educational Series, 1978.

Bayer, Patricia, ed. *The Fine Art of the Furniture Maker.* Rochester, N.Y.: Memorial Art Gallery of the University of Rochester, 1981.

Bethune, James, P. *Technical Illustration.* New York: John Wiley & Sons, Inc., 1983.

Bradford, Peter. *Chair, The Current State of the Art.* New York: Thomas Y. Crowell Publishers, 1978.

Branzi, Andrea. *The Hot House: Italian New Wave Design.* Cambridge, Mass: MIT Press, 1984.

Brooks, Vicki. *Portable Furniture.* Pittstown, N.J.: The Main Street Press, 1986.

Burgman, Harry. *The Pen and Pencil Technique Book.* New York: Watson-Guptill Publications, 1984.

Camard, Florence. *Ruhlmann: Master of Art Deco.* Paris: Editions du Regard, 1983.

Chippendale, Thomas. *The Gentleman & Cabinet-Maker's Director.* Reprint of 3rd ed. New York: Dover Publications, Inc., 1966.

Clifford, Martin. *Basic Drafting.* Blue Ridge Summit, Pa.: Tab Books, 1980.

Cooper-Hewitt Museum. *Scandinavian Modern Design.* New York: Harry N. Abrams, Inc., 1982.

Croney, John. *Anthropometrics for Designers.* New York: Van Nostrand Reinhold Co., 1971.

Dalisi, Riccardo. *Gaudi: Furniture and Objects.* Woodbury, N.Y.: Barron's Educational Series, 1980.

D'Amelio, Joseph. *Perspective Drawing Handbook.* New York: Van Nostrand Reinhold, 1984.

De Fusco, Renato. *Le Corbusier, Designer—Furniture, 1929.* Woodbury, N.Y.: Barron's Educational Series, 1977.

Diffrient, Niels, Alvin R. Tilley and Joan C. Bardagjy. *Humanscale 1/2/3.* Cambridge, Mass.: MIT Press, 1974.

Domergue, Denise. *Artists Design Furniture.* New York: Harry N. Abrams, Inc., 1984.

Drexler, Arthur. *Charles Eames: Furniture From the Design Collection.* New York: Museum of Modern Art, 1973.

Fox, Judith H. *Furniture, Furnishings: Subject and Object.* Providence, R.I.: Rhode Island School of Design, 1984.

Garner, Philippe. *Twentieth-Century Furniture.* New York: Van Nostrand Reinhold Co., 1980.

Hambidge, Jay. *Elements of Dynamic Symmetry.* New York: Dover Publications, 1967.

Hanks, David A. *Innovative Furniture in America.* New York: Horizon Press, 1981.

Hennessey, James and Victor J. Papanek. *Nomadic Furniture.* New York: Pantheon Books, 1973.

Hennessey, James and Victor J. Papanek. *Nomadic Furniture 2.* New York: Pantheon Books, 1974.

Hohauser, Sanford. *Architectural and Interior Models.* New York: Van Nostrand Reinhold Co., 1984.

Huntley, H.E. *Divine Proportion.* New York: Dover Publications, 1970.

Itten, Johannes. *Elements of Color.* New York: Van Nostrand Reinhold Co., 1970.

Jensen, Robert and Patricia Conway. *Ornamentalism.* New York: Clarkson N. Potter, 1982.

Kemnitzer, Ronald B. *Rendering with Markers.* New York: Watson-Guptill Publications, 1983.

Kepes, Gyorgy. *Module, Proportion, Symmetry, Rhythm.* New York: George Braziller, 1966.

Lopez, Ulises M. and George E. Warrin. *Mechanical Drawing.* Reston, Va.: Reston Publishing Co., 1984.

Museum of Finnish Architecture, Finnish Society of Crafts and Design, Artek. *Alvar Aalto Furniture.* Cambridge, Mass.: The MIT Press, 1985.

Page, Marian. *Furniture Designed by Architects.* New York: Whitney Library of Design, 1983.

Panero, Julius. *Anatomy for Interior Designers.* 3rd ed. New York: Whitney Library of Design, 1962.

Panero, Julius and Martin Zelnik. *Human Dimension and Interior Space.* New York: Whitney Library of Design, 1979.

Pennick, Nigel. *Sacred Geometry.* Great Britain: Turnstone Press, 1980.

Philadelphia Museum of Art. *Design Since 1945.* Philadelphia: Philadelphia Museum of Art, 1983.

Pye, David. *The Nature and Aesthetics of Design.* New York: Van Nostrand Reinhold Co., 1982.

Pye, David. *The Nature and Aesthetics of Workmanship.* Cambridge, England, and New York: Cambridge University Press, 1968.

Radice, Barbara. *Memphis.* New York: Rizzoli International Publications, Inc., 1985.

Ramsey, Charles and Harold Sleeper. *Architectural Graphic Standards.* 7th ed. New York: John Wiley & Sons, Inc., 1981.

Ratensky, Alexander. *Drawing and Modelmaking.* New York: Whitney Library of Design, 1983.

Simpson, Thomas. *Fantasy Furniture.* New York: Reinhold Book Corp., 1968.

Sprigg, June. *Shaker Design.* New York: Whitney Museum of American Art, 1986.

Wang, Thomas C. *Pencil Sketching.* New York: Van Nostrand Reinhold Co., 1977.

Whitney Museum. *High Styles: Twentieth-Century American Design.* New York: Whitney Museum of American Art, 1985.

Wilk, Christopher. *Thonet: 150 Years of Furniture.* Woodbury, N.Y.: Barron's Educational Series, Inc., 1980.

magazines

Abitare. Editrice Abitare, Segesta s.P.a., 15 Corso Monforte, 20122 Milan, Italy.

American Craft. 45 W. 45th St., New York, N.Y. 10019.

Architectural Digest. Architectural Digest Publishing Corp., 5900 Wilshire Blvd., Los Angeles, Calif. 90036.

Architectural Record. 1221 Avenue of the Americas, New York, N.Y. 10020.

Crafts. Crafts Council, 8 Waterloo Place, London, England SW1 4AT.

Design. The Design Council, 28 Haymarket, London, England SW1Y 4SU.

Designer's Journal. The Architectural Press, 9 Queen Anne's Gate, London, England SW1H 9BY.

Domus. Editoriale Domas s.P.a., c/o Speedimpex USA, Inc., 45-45 39th St., Long Island City, N.Y. 11104.

Fine Woodworking. The Taunton Press, 63 S. Main St., P.O. Box 355, Newtown, Conn. 06470.

Furniture Design & Manufacturing. 400 N. Michigan Ave., Suite 1216, Chicago, Ill. 60611.

Furniture Today. 200 S. Main St., P.O. Box 2754, High Point, N.C. 27261.

Industrial Design. 330 W. 42nd St., New York, N.Y. 10036.

Interior Design. Cahners Publishing, 475 Park Ave. S., New York, N.Y. 10022.

Interiors. Billboard Publications, 1515 Broadway, New York, N.Y. 10036.

MD (Moebel Design). Postfach 10 02 52, 7022 Leinfelden-Echterdingen, W. Germany.

Metropolis. Bellerophon Publications, 177 E. 87th St., New York, N.Y. 10128.

Metropolitan Home. 750 Third Ave., New York, N.Y. 10017.

Model Railroader. Kalmbach Publishing, 1027 North 7th St., Milwaukee, Wis. 53233.

Progressive Architecture. 600 Summer St., Stamford, Conn. 06904.

index

senior editor	Paul Bertorelli
designer/layout artist	Ben Kann
art assistants	Iliana Koehler, Cindy Nyitray
copy/production editor	Ruth Dobsevage
typesetter	Nancy-Lou Knapp
print production manager	Peggy Dutton
indexer	Harriet Hodges

typeface	ITC Garamond Book
paper	Mountie Matte, 70 lb., neutral pH
printer and binder	Arcata Graphics/Hawkins, New Canton, Tennessee